Writing in the Social Studies

Writing in the Social Studies

A Practical Guide for Teaching an Essential Skill

Aaron Pribble

ROWMAN & LITTLEFIELD
Lanham • Boulder • New York • London

Published by Rowman & Littlefield
An imprint of The Rowman & Littlefield Publishing Group, Inc.
4501 Forbes Boulevard, Suite 200, Lanham, Maryland 20706
www.rowman.com

6 Tinworth Street, London SE11 5AL, United Kingdom

British Library Cataloguing in Publication Information Available

Library of Congress Cataloging-in-Publication Data

Names: Pribble, Aaron, 1980- author.
Title: Writing in the social studies : a practical guide for teaching an essential skill / Aaron Pribble.
Description: Lanham, Maryland : Rowman & Littlefield, 2021. | Includes bibliographical references. | Summary: "Writing in the Social Studies is a practical guide for educators. On each page are strategies, tips, and takeaways for teachers to implement in their classroom, while every chapter concludes with helpful handouts to distribute directly to students. Beginning with a framework and pacing guide, Writing in the Social Studies examines foundational, academic, and real-world writing, concluding with a methodology for grading and a spirited plea for teachers to write themselves. Teachers who believe in teaching "skills through content" finally have a blueprint from which to work. Those who understand it is imperative students graduate with the ability to think critically and express a point of view now have a vehicle with which to achieve their goals. Writing in the Social Studies will be the first book to tackle this crucial yet neglected corner of the curriculum. There is a desperate need for professional development in this area, and therefore also tremendous opportunity. It is a professional imperative that social studies educators teach a variety of writing skills through content. As a result they should have access to a resource which clearly and engagingly shows them how. This is Writing in the Social Studies"—Provided by publisher.
Identifiers: LCCN 2020053441 (print) | LCCN 2020053442 (ebook) | ISBN 9781475859102 (cloth) | ISBN 9781475859119 (paperback) | ISBN 9781475859126 (epub)
Subjects: LCSH: Social sciences—Study and teaching (Secondary) | Composition (Language arts)—Study and teaching (Secondary) | Language arts—Correlation with content subjects.
Classification: LCC H62 .P668 2021 (print) | LCC H62 (ebook) | DDC 300.71/2—dc23
LC record available at https://lccn.loc.gov/2020053441
LC ebook record available at https://lccn.loc.gov/2020053442

Focus on the process.

—Coach Alex Pribble

For Jackie, born around the same time as this book

Contents

Preface

I was flipping through a cookbook about tacos with my family in a knick-knack shop in Olympia, Washington, when the idea for an altogether different type of book overtook me like a hunger. Inspired by the chef's how-to guide, part musings and provocation, part argument for and exploration of his professional passion, I decided to do the same for mine: teaching writing in social studies. There in that store I was inspired to assemble a guide for fellow teachers, a series of recipes for writing in a discipline that demands it yet offers little in the way of support.

Having spent the better part of two decades in the classroom immersed in everything from imperialism to opportunity cost to the American Revolution, I am particularly enthusiastic about the notion of teaching skills like writing through a variety of social studies content. Yet I've looked and researched and scoured and uncovered but a few resources for this subject when in fact there ought to be many. So I decided to create one, bringing together the numerous ingredients involved in teaching social studies writing.

It's been my experience that the best professional development has come horizontally, from fellow teachers. I've learned much from my school and district department colleagues as well as from social studies friends across the country, and I'd like to return the favor. I want to share whatever knowledge I've acquired—and hopefully someday you will too. In that spirit *Writing in the Social Studies* is offered as a book for teachers, by a teacher.

Over the years I have also found there never quite seems to be enough time during the school day for this type of work. Department meetings, prep periods, chats in the hall between classes never suffice. For example, I've been engaged in an on-and-off debate for multiple years running with my erstwhile English teaching partner about how to properly construct a thesis. The following pages are at least in part a response to him and a reflection of my yearning for a larger and more sustained conversation rather than inter-mittent bursts of dialogue. Maybe you have felt the same.

This book is concerned with *how* to teach writing in social studies but let's start with the *why*. Why do it? Because writing not only allows students to clearly and persuasively communicate their ideas but also helps them think. Writing actually makes us smarter, sharpening our mental powers of analysis, organization, and observation whether in service to more fully real-izing our human potential or simply being a superior employee at work. Plus social studies' gripping content presents a rich opportunity through which to practice this all-important skill (and as we'll see, practice is the only way to achieve any semblance of perfection).

Even if that's true isn't writing still the purview of English? Nonfiction writing is part of the English curriculum, yes, but certainly not exclusively. If you think of the most popular and influential books at any given time, my suspicion is that a preponderance of them will be social studies-related. The writing of historians, sociologists, geographers, anthropologists, psycholo-gists, economists, and political scientists all fall within the purview of social studies, and therefore we should all be actively encouraging our students to write.

The aim of this book is to show them how. And since all good writing seeks to engage and inform, rather than a textbook I envision these pages as an enjoyable guide, a collection of ideas intended to offer a path forward whether you're toward the beginning, middle, or end of your career. I hope the following will provoke you, whet your appetite for teaching writing, make you think about our discipline in a new way, and ultimately lead to greater student learning and a generation of more able nonfiction writers.

Lost in thought in the knick-knack shop, I heard a voice call out and real-ized I was being summoned. I put down the cookbook midway through a disquisition on homemade corn tortillas and hustled out the door, taking with me only inspiration. Upon my return to San Francisco, however, I discovered a compostably wrapped rectangular gift resting on the kitchen table. It seems someone had taken notice of my interest and was demonstrating their familial affection. Or at the very least their love of eating tacos.

Little did they know that book had given me so much more.

Acknowledgments

I would first like to thank Tom Koerner, my editor at Rowman & Littlefield. After working with Tom on subsequent projects, I continue to find his advice sensible and discerning, and I appreciate his vision for what a book can ultimately become. I'd also like to thank Carlie Wall for her meticulous attention and care from start to finish. She has been a steady hand and a repository of valuable information.

I am indebted to my friends and colleagues Sharilyn Scharf, Augusto Andres, and Nate Bernstein for reading drafts of the manuscript and offering thoughtful guidance. True teachers, their feedback was incisive, useful, and consistently on the mark. We all know the school year is perpetually busy and their generosity will always mean a lot to me.

Thanks as well to the Social Studies Department at Tamalpais High School and across the entire Tamalpais Union High School District. Many of the ideas contained in this book I have learned from you. The countless conversations we've had about writing inform my own practice as well as the pages that follow.

Finally, my wife, Michelle, who more than anyone else has inspired me to transform what began as a conversation with myself, then with her, into something real. As I write, she is reading on the couch with her feet under a blanket, and I could not be more grateful for her presence in my life.

Introduction

As the title suggests, this book is a guide to help social studies teachers teach writing. This is not a grammar index; there will be no mention of adverbial clauses, conjunctive adverbs, or prepositional phrases. It's difficult to avoid any whisper of syntax or style when dealing with the study of language but rest assured we will hew closely to the pragmatic. Not a page should turn without there being something tangible for you to try in class tomorrow.

To that end, a list of bulleted key points concludes each chapter. Most chapters also include handouts for your individual use. Intellectual property considerations aside—and let's be real, who has the chutzpah to copyright their own curriculum—please feel free to photocopy and distribute the handouts to students. Do so as is or make digital copies and tweak them to your personal liking (maybe have a teacher's assistant type up the handouts to save time or find an app that quickly does the same).

Chapter 1, "The Framework," lays out a template for teaching writing in addition to a pacing guide and skills progression. This chapter is about the mindset, the approach, and it informs all others that follow. Without a comprehensive strategy for teaching writing, we might as well be throwing darts in the dark. While potentially enjoyable, it's certainly less effective.

Chapter 2, "Writing Is Thinking," illustrates the many indirect ways writing is manifested in the learning process and vice versa, including annotating, notetaking, and reading. These skills might not be considered writing per se, but they most certainly belong to the same family and play an integral role.

Chapter 3 is titled "Foundational Writing" and it describes the fundamentals of writing in the social studies. Knowing how to shape summaries and analytical paragraphs as well as how to evaluate the legitimacy of primary and secondary sources are essential building blocks for students. Without them it would be difficult if not impossible to write effectively in our discipline. We must all learn to walk before we can run, and writing is no different.

Chapters 4 and 5, "Academic Writing Part I" and "Academic Writing Part II," comprise the heart of what is typically conceived of as social studies writing: the process paper, the thesis, analytical essays, document-based questions, and, of course, the mother of them all—the research paper. These chapters also tackle the merit of the five-paragraph essay and the similarities and differences between writing in class and at home.

Chapter 6, "Real-World Writing," borders on the joyful—and for some students may even approximate fun. Designing assignments which exist outside the classroom such as op-eds, book reviews, essays of historical fiction, magazine features and profiles, white papers, legal briefs, family history research, memoirs, speeches, visual essays, and comics is about as relevant as social studies can get. "Real-World Writing" makes the case for the primacy of nonfiction and the salience of authentic assessment, and argues that such assignments offer the promise of at once boosting students' confidence and encouraging a love of writing.

The final chapter, "Writing as Assessment," addresses specifically how to grade as well as the philosophy surrounding why one should. It presents grading's underlying principles and goals, reviews the relative value of authentic versus academic and formative versus summative assessment, details the granular mechanics of grading writing, and concludes with a spirited plea both to separate scholastic achievement from moral worth and to emphasize the importance of mental toughness and positive psychology.

The epilogue, "Teachers Are Writers," argues that we ourselves should be writing. Not only will we improve our teaching practice, we'll also gain the same advantages as our students. We'll sharpen our thinking, enhance our communication skills, and learn to embrace ambiguity in complex ideas. From keeping a journal to maintaining a blog, writing can be as personal or as public as you like. Ideally it will be both. The world needs to hear from good teachers about the hidden truths of our profession; too often people speak for us and it's time we begin speaking for ourselves.

Lastly, I can't help mentioning the epigraphs[1] which begin each chapter. Many originate from my favorite books about writing and highlighting them on the following pages as well as in the suggested reading list is my way of showing deference to authors whose work has been meaningful in my own career. And if I'm being truly honest, it's also an attempt to join their ethereal conversation about the joys and virtues of writing. It's my wish that this book helps you do the same with your students.

NOTE

1. As opposed to epitaphs, as my English colleague and friend once mistakenly wrote in a letter home to parents.

Chapter 1

The Framework

Process over product.
　　　　　　　—Anonymous

I. A TEMPLATE

When teaching writing, the framework, or underlying structure, reigns supreme. It lords over the entire process—everything from daily assignments to unit assessments, determining their size, scope, and even their success. One might say the framework *is* the process. The core idea here is to determine how often you will teach writing and how frequently you'll provide students the opportunity to practice. Writing is a skill and skills take repetition to master. When teaching almost any skill, the following template applies:

　Explain, model, practice, give feedback, practice.

This is especially true of writing. Let's say you're teaching how to write an analytical paragraph (we'll address this in detail later). First explain what an analytical paragraph is and what's expected of students, usually with an assignment descriptor. Take as much time as you'd like formatting the perfect handout, but remember after the class reads it some will file the paper neatly away, others will jam it inside their backpack or forget it altogether, and a few, if you're lucky, will leave your hard work behind as a rough approximation of origami.

　The explanation portion of the process is no doubt important, but teachers often spend hours crafting a flawless descriptor only to see it languish on the classroom floor once students are dismissed. But fear not—this is merely step one.

Next provide a model. A model might be student writing samples or a more authentic selection from a newspaper or academic journal. Better yet offer both so that students can see how what they're doing in the classroom genuinely translates to real life. Have students read the models and discuss with a partner the ways in which they exemplify a sound analytical paragraph. Then debrief as a class, highlighting what you believe are the most important words, sentences, phrases, or sections. You might even refer students back to your beautifully styled artisanal handout.

Now is the fun part, the application. Students should practice what they've just learned, writing analytical paragraphs of their own. Walk the room and give informal oral feedback. When students are finished, they can trade with a partner for peer editing and feedback from a friend. You can also collect their writing for a more formal accounting of their strengths and weakness, and your feedback can come with or without a rubric and a grade (more on assessment later as well).

Once students have practiced a particular type of writing and have digested your notes on their performance, they should practice that type of writing again. And again and again as often as possible. There really is no substitute for the doing, the practice. If you have ever tried to master a skill yourself like in sports or music, this idea should make intuitive sense.

So to review:

Explain, model, practice, give feedback, practice.

This template is effective for mastery in general, but especially writing, and can be applied throughout the year.

II. PACING

How much practice is enough? Where and when will you find time for extra practice among the countless demands of the curriculum? There are no simple answers to these questions but in short: *aim to practice writing every week if not every day.* As you'll see, there are myriad and seemingly infinite varieties of social studies writing, and so if students put paper to pencil, or fingers to keyboard, odds are they will be practicing something.

One concrete example is WAR, or weekly academic writing. That the acronym works only phonetically is a humorous witticism you can share with your students. Add a wry smile and see which of your kids are cool (cool being defined as anyone who will laugh at your jokes). Try making WAR a regular part of your week, say every Monday. As an added benefit, if you don't feel like much direct instruction on the first day back from your weekend great—it's time for student writing. They know the drill, it's part of the routine, they can expect it.

If this feels too rigid, then simply keep a mental goal of students writing once per week or even once per day. At the end of each unit, students should also produce a more formal piece of writing to serve as one of your summative assessments (again more on grading later). For example, if students have been practicing analytical paragraphs for four to six weeks, it makes sense that as part of an exam they write one or two or three to demonstrate the extent to which they've mastered the form.

Finally, remember that skills and content are not mutually exclusive. By teaching *skills through content* students are practicing the former while learning the latter. Devoting one more class period to writing is not one less for subject matter; the theme of the analytical paragraphs will necessarily be the content objectives of the day. In this way, writing serves to augment rather than diminish student knowledge.

III. SKILLS PROGRESSION

Now that we have a general awareness of the template for teaching writing and an idea about how often this should occur let's consider explicitly what to teach and when. While the progression need not be as linear or lockstep as in mathematics, for example, it's nonetheless sensible to stack skills whenever possible. Think about which are absolutely fundamental and which are applied, those necessary to walk and those required to run. Consider this progression:

> *Annotating; notetaking; summary; source analysis; analytical paragraph; thesis; analytical essay; document-based question; research paper.*

From back to front, it's evident that a research paper requires the ability to acquire and evaluate sources, summarize, and make and defend an argument, so it makes sense to teach those skills in succession (in fact, the reminder of the book is structured in just this way).

Once you establish roughly how much time per week you're able to devote to writing, you can then think about what *type* of writing you'd like your students to do. For example, you might spend the first week teaching how to annotate a text and the next week how to take notes—both technically reading strategies, yes, but also integral to writing.

For the rest of the year, students will be practicing these skills for homework or in class. The third week you might teach students how to write a summary, remembering to provide plenty of time for practice. Maybe unit one ends here and you ask students to write a summary paragraph as part of their summative assessment.

And so on. The next unit students learn how to write analytical paragraphs, the unit after that they write analytical essays followed by document-based essays, concluding with the apotheosis of social studies writing: the research paper. Think about all the writing skills you'd like students to learn in your class over the course of the year then back into them, teaching each in succession with ample practice.

Without a plan of attack, lacking an idea of what you want students to learn and when, the year can seem like a haphazard romp through one's curriculum. Knowing that by summer students will learn a discrete and valuable set of writing skills, however, gives your class an intellectual anchor, a rudder, and a compass as you guide them along the way. So sail forth, mighty captain, and chart the most effective course for teaching writing through your social studies content.

KEY IDEAS

- Use the writing template as your process: explain, model, practice, give feedback, practice.
- Practice writing as much as you can in class, like every week or every day.
- Plan your skills progression for the year, such as annotating, notetaking, summary, source analysis, analytical paragraph, thesis, analytical essay, document-based question, and research paper.

Chapter 2

Writing Is Thinking

We have all seized the white perimeter as our own
and reached for a pen if only to show
we did not just laze in an armchair turning pages;
we pressed a thought into the wayside,
planted an impression along the verge.

—*Marginalia*, Billy Collins

You can't be a good writer without being a devoted reader.

—J.K. Rowling

I. ANNOTATING

Reading is easier than writing. One requires passive thought, the other active. If you have ever attempted to learn a foreign language, for example, you were undoubtedly better able to understand through listening and reading than you were able to produce language as speech or prose. This is because taking in information is less challenging for the mind than churning it out. Inputs precede outputs. (Envision here a quote from a formidable cognitive neuroscientist, perhaps one who has just published a major longitudinal study confirming this assertion.)

In other words, reading and writing share a dynamic relationship in the brain, operating jointly for the purposes of intellectual development. Likewise in social studies, teaching reading strategies is an essential part of teaching writing. And a nice place to start is with annotation, a magical and often addictive pursuit. Annotation flips the equation, transmuting reading from passive to active thought, demonstrating visually the internal workings of the active reader. If you yourself find it difficult to read without a pen or pencil in hand, scribbling in the margins and between lines of a text, you might be an addict. Welcome to the club!

Simply put, to annotate means to mark up a text. For the etymologically inclined "annotate" derives from the Latin verb *annotare* meaning "to mark." Annotating therefore is just taking notes on the text itself rather than a separate page. It can and should, however, involve a number of related techniques:

Highlighting or underlining phrases or sentences; boxing or circling key words; placing stars, question marks, exclamation points, brackets, symbols, drawings in the margins; writing summaries, connections, questions, feelings, opinions in the margins.

Students should highlight or underline passages they deem important which, believe it or not, requires elevated thinking to rank the salience of ideas. Plus highlighting or underlining means reading over words a second time, furthering retention. But be warned: highlighting alone is insufficient and should be complemented by other marginalia in pen or pencil, even if students prefer the eye-grabbing neon of the Sharpie. For those not using a highlighter, one writing utensil will suffice.

Boxing key words is tantamount to bolded words in a textbook, signaling to the reader their importance. As an added benefit, one's eyes are drawn to the boxes popping from the page. This is especially useful during class discussions as well as for review or when writing a response. Same goes for circling, which indicates an unknown word or a problem, conflict, or disagreement with the author.

In the margins of a text the meanings of stars, exclamation points, and question marks are unambiguous and should be used liberally. Brackets can indicate an important section—but not so important as to earn an underline or highlight (the bracket is the lazy person's shortcut, especially during a skim or quick-read). Symbols and images are also a nice way to concisely represent an idea. A simple pyramid might denote inequality or rigid class structure, for example, while a boat floating along waves, well, you get the drift. Student drawings might even make annotating *fun*.

Finally, students should write in the margins what comes to mind. This might be a brief summary of the passage, a reaction like Huh or Gross!, a question, disagreement, or personal connection. The point here is to *engage* with the text. If books themselves can be understood as links in a larger conversation chain, then writing in the margins allows students to converse directly with the author, to argue, empathize, or exclaim, contemplate, critique, and compare. Annotation brings texts to life. It morphs reading from passive into active thought. And most important, it's a key reading strategy that will help students learn how to write.

II. NOTETAKING

Like annotating, notetaking is a way for students to engage with a reading. Students can take notes from other inputs like films and lectures, of course, but our focus here is on reading strategies.

Conceptually, good notes organize and synthesize information, making a subject easier for students to comprehend. The two most important features of any notetaking system are *big ideas* and *supporting details*. We'll discuss a few methods specifically but know that the options are nearly limitless. Consider explicitly teaching several notetaking systems, say one per week over the first three to four weeks, then once students demonstrate proficiency give them the option of using their favorite(s) for the remainder of the year. Along with annotation, they'll come away with a handful of helpful skills for digesting a text.

The gold standard of notetaking is without question the Cornell Method. Yes, it was indeed invented at Cornell, by an education professor named Walter Pauk in the mid-twentieth century. The left third of the page contains main ideas and the right two-thirds supporting details. When finished, students write a summary of the section as a whole.

Cornell Notes are simple and effective but keep in mind a few subtle points. Students should write identifying information at the top of their paper like their name, the date, the class period, and the corresponding title and page numbers of the reading. They should also build their notes in such a way that the main idea on the left aligns visually across the page with the supporting details on the right. And though some advocate a summary at the bottom of each physical—or digital—page, one summary at the end of the entire section is both more efficient and effective.

A handout is included at the end of the chapter. Consider pairing it with an exemplary student model, perhaps even good, bad, and average models so your classes can appraise a range of student work.

Another potent notetaking method is called Headline-Question (HQ). As the name suggests, HQ Notes involve turning the headline of a section into a question and then answering that question with an answer. That's it. While Cornell Notes use bullet points, HQ Notes are written in narrative form like a summary paragraph. The first sentence should address the question and main idea directly, and the remaining sentences should provide an appropriate amount of supporting detail.

Key to HQ Notes is formulating a question that allows for an answer which fully and completely illustrates the most important elements of a section. What, how, and why should be used precisely and when necessary together. Though HQ Notes work well for articles and essays with prominent section headings, they're particularly effective when taking notes from a textbook. See the handout at the end of the chapter, and don't forget to pair with an exemplar.

Finally, the ever-present outline notetaking method. The default, the common denominator, the technique so pervasive it does not even require a proper noun. You know the form: roman numerals on the first line followed by numbers indented on the second, letters further indented on the third, and so on.

The advantage of this method is that indentations show a clear subordinating of information. One can view the top-line main idea and follow subsequent indentations down to increasingly specific details. While outlining may be the most ubiquitous style of notetaking, it's actually quite difficult since every indentation indicates a necessarily lower-ranking idea, a mental exercise some students may find taxing and therefore renounce altogether.

Other forms of notetaking exist as well. The Note Take-Note Make method, like a dialectical journal, directs students to take notes on the left half of the page while writing their own thoughts and opinions on the right; the One Pager method requires students take all notes on one page only, with a headline and symbolic image surrounded by clustered notes at the top and questions with answers at bottom. Both are respectable strategies in their own right and are evidence of the many different configurations notes might take.

Save for one. The uniquely verboten, embryonic echo of the genuine form, the bulleted list. Please *do not* allow students merely to tick off shorthand down a page in whatever haphazard order and fashion they desire. The bulleted list is wrong for the simple reason others are right: because it lacks a way to distinguish between main ideas and supporting details—an overlooked but essential element in taking notes. (In fairness, bullets can be an appropriate differentiation for students who need extra support and a more simplified scheme.)

Whichever style students eventually decide they prefer, even if they choose to create an altogether new method themselves, it's imperative that a notetaking system has three things: *the proper identifying heading, a space for main ideas, and a slightly larger space for subordinate supporting details.* Summary and personal opinion are attractive but inessential features also worthy of consideration. And in the end whatever methods you ultimately decide to teach, beware the bulleted list.

III. READING AND WRITING

A closing thought: good readers make good writers. Students should be encouraged to read for a variety of reasons—for the sheer joy, for the sharpening of the mind, to better understand our world—and also because those who read frequently know what good writing sounds like. They can appreciate the rhythm of a paragraph, the beat of a well-metered sentence, the tone of an alliterated phrase. It's no guarantee, of course, but if you want to become a writer, other than writing the best thing you can do is to read.

KEY IDEAS

- Annotating and notetaking are active reading strategies that are an essential part of teaching writing.
- To annotate is to mark up the words and margins of a text.
- Effective notetaking systems organize and synthesize information, distinguishing between main ideas and supporting details.

How to Annotate a Text

Annotate: to mark, note, interpret, or explain.

Annotating is an active reading strategy that helps you make meaning of a text. Almost like having a conversation with it.

Sample annotation techniques:

• Underline or highlight important sentences and phrases
• Box key terms
• Circle unknown words
• Put a star or asterisk next to critical ideas and main points
• Put a question mark next to things about which you have a question
• Write your opinion in the margins
• Write questions in the margins
• Write summaries in the margins
• Make connections to other stuff in the margins
• Draw other relevant symbols or images in the margins

Other ideas:

• Color code your annotations if that's your thing
• Bracket several lines that seem important and draw a vertical line down the margin
• Use acronyms like VIP, OMG, SMH, WTF, etc.
• Use other symbols that make sense to you like triangles, squiggly lines, etc.

Cornell Notetaking Method

Fun fact! Cornell Notes were invented at Cornell University by an education professor named Walter Pauk in the 1940s. Cornell Notes are in many ways the gold standard of all notetaking methods. They're clean, effective, and easy to use. On the left third of the page, write main ideas. On the right two-thirds of the page, write important supporting details. When you're finished, include a summary of the entire section at the end. That's it.

A few tips:

• Make sure your supporting details align visually with your main ideas
• The main ideas column can include symbols and images instead of words
• Details can be written however you'd like—in paragraphs, short sentences, or bullets
• Don't forget to include a title as well as your name, the date, and the period
• Write your summary at the end of all your notes, not the bottom of each page

Take Cornell notes in the space below as practice.

Headline-Question Notetaking Method

The HQ notetaking strategy is fairly self-explanatory. Turn the headline of a reading section into a question and then answer the question. This method works particularly well for readings with clearly "chunked" headings such as textbooks.

A few things to keep in mind:

- Write your answers in narrative paragraphs rather than bullet points
- Make sure your first sentence directly and succinctly answers the question
- Put the answer into your own words (paraphrase, don't copy word-for-word)
- Confirm your question directly addresses the content of the section
- Think about reading the section first before writing your question

Use these helpful words when turning the headline into a question:

- How; Why; What; Who; When; Where

Consider the examples below.

Headline: Cold War Origins
Question: What were the origins of the Cold War?
    Or
Question: How did the Cold War begin?
Headline: Fearing the Influence of Communists
Question: Why were Americans afraid of communism in the United States?
    Or
Question: How did a fear of communism affect the freedom of Americans?
Remember—your question should allow for an answer that fully, accurately, and completely addresses the reading passage. Be thoughtful about how you write your questions.

Outline Notetaking Method

There are a number of ways to take notes. Perhaps the most traditional is by making an outline. What's important to know is that each indentation signals a *subordination* of information. In other words, main ideas will be found to the left of the page and supporting details, those less important or more specific, will be indented below and to the right.

For example:

   I. Main idea
      A. Supporting detail
         1. Supporting detail of the supporting detail
            a) Supporting detail of the supporting detail of the supporting detail

Note that all three supporting details—A., 1., and a)—relate back to the initial main idea.

Your notes might also look like this:

   I. Main idea
      A. Supporting detail
      B. Supporting detail
         1. Supporting detail
      C. Supporting detail
  II. Main idea
      A. Supporting detail

How you choose to subordinate or rank information is up to you (remember this is an important critical thinking skill in and of itself).

Chapter 3

Foundational Writing

Prose is a human exchange between writer and reader. Everything consigned to the page needs to ring true.

—*Sin and Syntax*, Constance Hale

I. STYLE

Though style is predominantly the domain of English, it is still an aspect of writing with which social studies teachers should be familiar. English teachers rightly emphasize style in their courses to a much greater extent than do social studies teachers—even those who regularly teach writing. If style is the grist of the English teacher's mill, in social studies it's more like the chaff.

So even though you likely won't spend time dissecting the details of participial phrases and dangling modifiers, you can still encourage students to find their voice on the page. Authenticity and individuality are core components of adolescence, and tying these ideals to self-expression is an effective way of exciting students about the writing process.

Here metaphor can be effective. Compare one's writing style to their sense of style with clothes. In the same way students reveal their identity through a particular look, by pairing shoes, shirts and accessories just so, they can also combine words, sentences, and phrases in a manner that represents who they are. Teenagers want to be themselves (while never straying too far from the pack) and they can communicate in words what they also say with fashion.

Beyond explanation and encouragement, however, instruction around writing style is the dominion of our colleagues in English. You can introduce students to the guidelines of grammar, the wonders of word choice, and the way sentences sometimes flow like music, but do not feel the need to dive deeper. There is simply no extra space in our curriculum given the demands of teaching social studies skills and content—even if in their writing style we hope students find beauty, delight, and maybe also themselves.

II. SUMMARY

Before moving to analysis, which comprises the heart of social studies writing and much of the remainder of this book, it's necessary to briefly consider how to write a summary. Like taking notes, summarizing is actually an exacting mental exercise. It requires students to rank, subordinate, and synthesize information, determining what is important and what is not, what is necessary supporting detail and what is less than significant.

Like making a fine whiskey, distilling a chapter or article means reducing the material to its essential elements. (Contrary to fashion, this metaphor may be inappropriate for teenagers of course.) Students should understand that a summary:

Is paraphrased and shorter than the original content; includes the main idea and necessary supporting details; does not incorporate one's opinion.

But how much shorter than the original? Students will surely ask. To which you can reply with the Goldilocks rule: not too much or too little, just the right amount. For those who struggle with ambiguity, recommend one-third to one-fifth of the total length of the passage, one paragraph, or even one sentence. One-sentence summaries take great skill to write and are more challenging than logorrheic regurgitation. You might even experiment with one-word summaries at the beginning or end of class to instigate discussion.

Students will also occasionally insert quotes into summaries, but paraphrasing is superior because it helps with both comprehension and abbreviation alike. Opinion, too, is a red flag that one doesn't understand the form. Save opinion for analysis. If we ultimately want students to learn how to make and defend an argument, a necessary first step is appreciating how to summarize. How to sum up and boil down.

In summarizing as in life, less truly is more.

III. ANALYTICAL PARAGRAPHS

After training students to write summaries, a logical next step is teaching them how to write analytical paragraphs. Analytical paragraphs contain all the constituent features of an analytical essay but in simplified (or summarized!) form. The three essentials are:

Argument, evidence, and analysis.

Students should understand that analytical writing is opinion-oriented and that opinion writing requires an argument. A good argument should be clear and precise, and supported with evidence and analysis. (Students may be familiar with the terms "claim" and "thesis" which are generally synonymous though we'll discuss technical distinctions later.)

An argument is what the paragraph attempts to prove. "Harriet Tubman is an American hero"; "Pancakes are superior to waffles"; and "The weather outside is nice" are all arguments, while "Harriet Tubman's birth name was Araminta Ross"; "My family eats pancakes on Sundays"; and "The temperature on the field is seventy-five degrees" are not. The former must be substantiated with evidence while the later are facts. (Note: Using at least some non-social-studies-related examples can be an effective way of isolating the structure of an argument, so students are not distracted by its content.)

In an analytical paragraph, evidence is one of the two ways to validate an argument. Evidence is the proof. It can be qualitative, including quotes, examples, anecdotes, and other descriptive information, as well as quantitative, or statistics, numbers, measurements, and other material driven by data.

A quote from Vanderbilt University history professor and abolitionist movement expert Dr. Richard Blackett about Tubman's valor and legacy of fighting for equality would be an effective piece of qualitative evidence, as would a recounting of one of her nineteen trips to the South escorting others to freedom. Surveys of the percentage of Americans who agree she is a hero and the seventy enslaved people she delivered to the North, on the other hand, are both examples of quantitative evidence.

Ironically the analytical paragraph's eponym, analysis, is the concept with which students struggle most. Analysis explains how one's evidence supports one's argument, detailing what the evidence shows, what it means, why it's significant. Analysis completes the loop, returning an analytical paragraph back to the argument with which it started.

Word stems signaling analysis are often of immense benefit to students. They include the following:

Thus, therefore, then, so, hence, accordingly, consequently, as a consequence, as result, in this way, this shows.

"Dr. Blackett's quote clearly demonstrates Harriet Tubman is an American hero." "That Tubman rescued over 70 African Americans from slavery shows she is worthy of our national admiration and praise." These stem words and phrases will shove hesitant students down the mountain, rendering inevitable their tumble toward analysis.

Analytical paragraphs themselves can take two forms: woven and straight. The latter, in which students write their argument, then all their evidence, then conclude with analysis, is simple and direct. The former calls for threading analysis around each piece of evidence—argument, evidence, analysis, evidence, analysis, and so on—which is a more nuanced but not necessarily superior style of writing. (See the handout included at the end of this chapter for additional explanation and classroom use.)

By moving from summary to analytical paragraph writing, students are able to stack one skill on top of another. They progress from identifying a main idea and its supporting details to making and defending an argument of their own. Analytical paragraphs familiarize students with the concepts of argument, evidence, and analysis before they advance to more challenging tasks like entire argumentative essays. And with ample practice even the research paper, the holy grail of social studies writing, will not appear daunting at all.

IV. SOURCE ANALYSIS

Determining the veracity of sources is among the most important skills social studies teachers can impart to their students. Today's supersaturation of information has elevated the priority of synthesis and evaluation. The overabundance of knowledge means it's as important to distinguish *between* sources as it is to locate them in the first place. In every social studies course—from government to American history to geography to economics—we should teach students to be critical readers, thinkers, and, of course, critical writers.

Fortunately, source analysis is one area in which a number of excellent resources exist. Take, for example, the CRAAP Test developed by librarians at California State University in Chico. The acronym CRAAP stands for *currency, relevance, authority, accuracy,* and *purpose.* This helpful mnemonic device encourages students to assess several criteria when making a decision about the overall quality of a source.

When was the source created? Is it appropriate? Who wrote it? Is it true? What is it for? These simple questions nicely frame the process of source evaluation for students. After creating a CRAAP Test handout, you can ask students to analyze a variety of sources, listing the C-R-A-A-P for each. And if you dare, debrief by asking them to rank the "crappiness" of each source.

The Stanford History Education Group, or SHEG, has also created a number of instruments for evaluating sources—particularly historical ones. Their historical thinking chart, for example, breaks historical reading skills into *sourcing, contextualization, corroboration,* and *close reading.*

Students should think about not only who wrote the source and why (sourcing) but also the era in which it was created (contextualization), if other documents can verify its truthfulness (corroboration), and what the content is actually saying in the first place (close reading). Like the CRAAP Test, find a SHEG historical thinking chart or create one yourself, then have students use it in conjunction with various documents to practice their powers of historical source evaluation.

A final helpful aid is the Historical Thinking Project of the University of British Columbia. Of their "Bix Six" Historical Thinking Concepts—establish historical significance; use primary source evidence; identify continuity and change; analyze cause and consequence; take historical perspectives; and understand the ethical dimension of history—using primary sources is an especially key skill to develop in burgeoning historians as well as all young social studiers in general.

Primary sources should be read for historical context and not just as information. Mining sources for evidence, students should make inferences about the world and the time in which they were created.

While SHEG and the Historical Thinking Project emphasize primary source analysis, it's equally important for students to be critical connoisseurs of secondary sources too. In some ways the difference is simple, in other ways it's quite complex.

Students should know that a primary source is "firsthand" or "direct" and also that it was created *during a particular period of time.* Examples of primary sources include letters, diaries, journals, interviews, official government records, news articles, photographs, paintings, maps, novels, music, video, movies, text messages, emails, social media posts, and many more. Again, anything created at a certain moment in time.

Conversely, secondary sources contain commentary about primary sources. They're written after the fact and involve anything from analysis and evaluation to interpretation and summary. Secondary sources can be histories, essays, reviews, encyclopedias, articles, magazines, movies, etcetera—anything that comments on an erstwhile source.

You may notice that both lists are cross-pollinated. This is because a source can be both primary and secondary. The ubiquitous classroom textbook will contain both original document excerpts as well as second-hand expository writing from current experts in the field, a common example of primary and secondary sources in one. But also consider a newspaper article written in the 1950s. That article is a primary source today but was a secondary source back then. The secondary source of today, in other words, becomes the primary source of tomorrow.

If your students understand the basic differences between primary and secondary sources, that's great. If they understand the subtle chronological relationship between them, that's even better. And if they can determine the trustworthiness of sources primary and secondary alike, they will not only be better social studies students but also more able to navigate a world overflowing with information. A world where intelligence lies not as much in hunting for information as in sifting through and evaluating it.

Critical thinking involves the constant questioning of sources. Do they pass the CRAAP Test? What are their context and purpose? How do they serve my particular needs? Ultimately it's difficult for students to write well if they cannot think critically. And appreciating the reliability of a source, understanding if it is firsthand or interpretative, primary or secondary, is integral to this pursuit.

Source analysis is as fundamental a social studies skill as is the ability to craft summaries and analytical paragraphs. From here it's off to the races: students can begin writing full-length works like essays and research papers, which are the subjects of the following two chapters.

KEY IDEAS

• Though writing "style" is a much larger consideration in English class-rooms, it's worth mentioning in social studies as encouragement and perhaps even inspiration.
• A summary should shorten and paraphrase the original content, include the main idea and necessary supporting details, and exclude opinion.
• The three essential elements of an analytical paragraph are argument, evidence, and analysis.
• Students should be able to evaluate the trustworthiness of a source and determine if it is primary or secondary.

What Is Your Style?

When it comes to writing, a focus on "style" is more common in English than social studies. But we can at least keep the idea in the back of our minds. Regardless of the discipline or class, whenever we write, we are expressing ourselves. What we say is a reflection of who we are. If you care about being your authentic, individual self, you should therefore also care about how you write. This encompasses everything from the words you choose to the way you assemble them into sentences and paragraphs.

A good metaphor for writing style is fashion—or one's style of dress. Like it or not, wearing clothes (at least in public) is a requirement. So too is writing. Every time you leave your house, you are saying something with your attire. Similarly, every time you put words to the page or screen, you're also expressing who you are to those who read what you write. If your identity is important to you, if you care about the way you look, you should also care about the way you write. So let's learn about one from the other.

How would you describe your style of dress?	How would you describe your writing style?

How are your clothing and writing styles similar and how are they different?

What do the way you dress and the way you write say about your lifestyle in general?

How to Write a Summary

Like Goldilocks and the Three Bears, a good summary is about getting it just right. A summary should explain the main idea of a reading passage and include the appropriate amount of supporting detail—not too much or too little. Though it may seem simple, writing summaries can be deceptively difficult because you need to synthesize information and determine what is important and what is not. You need to distill a reading into its essence.

Keep in mind that a summary:

• Should be shorter than the original text (obviously)
• Should paraphrase the original text (your words, someone else's ideas)
• Should not include your own opinion (no analysis or argument)

How long is a summary? It depends. A summary can be one sentence, one page, one paragraph, or even one word. Sometimes summaries are one-third to one-fifth the length of the original reading. Most often we will write summaries in one paragraph.

Practice writing a one-word summary: _____

_____

_____

_____

Practice writing a one-sentence summary: _____

_____

_____

_____

_____

_____

Practice writing a one-paragraph summary: _____

_____

_____

_____

_____

_____

Finally, remember that summarizing is like life: sometimes less is more.

A Guide to Analytical Paragraph Writing

Analytical paragraphs are persuasive paragraphs that stand alone or are found in the body of a paper or essay. They have three main parts: argument, evidence, and analysis.

Argument: The point your paragraph is trying to prove or convey. Made clearly and precisely. If part of an essay, each argument should relate to your overall thesis.

Evidence: The proof used to substantiate your point. Can be qualitative (descriptive information like quotes, examples, and anecdotes). Can be quantitative (data-driven information like stats, numbers, and measurements).

Analysis: The explanation of how your evidence proves your argument. Comments on what your evidence shows, means, and why it's significant. Key words and phrases that signal analysis: thus, thusly, therefore, hence, consequently, as a consequence, accordingly, then, as a result, this shows, so, in this way, in this manner, in this fashion . . . (and many more!).

Analytical paragraphs usually take one of two forms.

#1 Straight

Begin with your argument, include all your evidence, finish with analysis. This style is simple and clear. Like this: argument, evidence, analysis.

#2 Woven

Begin with your argument, include a piece of evidence, weave in some analysis, include another piece of evidence, weave in more analysis, and so on and so forth until the paragraph is finished. This style is a bit more nuanced and advanced. Like this: argument, evidence, analysis, evidence, analysis, evidence, analysis.

Chapter 4

Academic Writing Part I

Writing affords us a luxury we lack in conversation: we can go back to recast our sentences, paying attention to syntax and sensuality in a way that's impossible when we're expounding extemporaneously—in speaking or in writing. And, paradoxically, when rewriting works, the prose sounds natural. It echoes our true voices.

—*Sin and Syntax*, Constance Hale

I. THE WRITING PROCESS

From start to finish there are a number of stages in the writing process, steps seasoned writers take naturally while neophytes rush or skip over altogether. In order they are:

Brainstorm, outline, write a first draft, revise, and polish.

Brainstorming can take many forms and occur across a variety of places and times. Nature walks, urban hikes, car rides, errands, chores, sleepless nights, eating, exercising—an opportunity for introspection is an opportunity to brainstorm. Ideas take time to percolate, to steep, settle, and brew, and sometimes one must sit—or walk or ride—with their thoughts, spend time with them, before an idea begins to take shape.

Once one's brain is sufficiently primed, it's necessary to make a record of the forthcoming ideas. Simply commit words to the page in any manner or form, listed in bullets, spewed like a blob, scribbled on shards of paper, tucked into a pocket, pecked out on a phone, dictated via talk-to-text

25

software, transcribed at a desk, as long as the result approximates the ideas swirling in your mind.

For greater structure, try creating a mind map or graphic organizer to more visually represent your thinking. If the subject is the First World War, for example, write "WWI" in the middle of the page and cluster ideas around it. If those ideas are related, draw arrowed lines until your document resembles a spider web. Or write "WWI" at the base of the page, adding words like branches on a tree until your paper blossoms in a canopy of unfolding thought. The main point of brainstorming—itself a wonderfully evocative word—is to record a writer's initial thoughts, to ready them like a lump of clay for future molding.

Whether brainstorming results from moments of solitary inspiration or anxious cramming, on paper, a screen, or purely in the mind, it's a crucial first step in the writing process, an investment which yields enormous dividends yet one that students often bypass in their haste to finish an assignment. Because of this, remember to explicitly create space in your lessons for students to brainstorm before beginning to write.

Outlining is the next step in the writing process and one with which students should be more familiar. Outlining transforms their embryonic ideas into a skeletal structure. Like notetaking methods, outlines appear in various formats, but all good outlines should *order and delineate ideas* so the author knows what's most important and what is supplementary.

After a proper heading, students can use roman numerals, numbers, letters, or any combination of symbols. Subordinated information will be indented below larger, more controlling ideas, all of which should be bound together by a thesis. Outlines can be sparse or dense according to one's needs, but they should lay out the contours of the entire work for the writer to grasp as a whole.

Completing an outline is a consequential, if enigmatic, accomplishment. Students can see the path ahead and should not despair of getting lost or making a wrong turn, but though the end is in sight, the real work has yet to begin. The journey of a thousand miles begins with a single step, as Lao Tzu's famed proverb suggests, and so each essay must also begin with a single word.

And thus we have arrived at the most tenuous juncture of the writing process. After several iterations of prewriting, it's now time to set off. At this point most adolescent writers, like writers in general, will look for any excuse to procrastinate. Students normally glued to a screen will find their attraction swiftly repelled like matching poles of two powerful magnets. Many are the bathrooms that have been visited, the doodles that have been drawn, the table partners who have been whispered to, all to avoid the tyranny of the blank page. The sheer terror of the unwritten word.

If the outline is a paper's skeleton, the first draft adds meat to its bones. It fleshes out the controlling ideas and gives them life. Beginning a first draft takes nothing short of herculean determination, yet there is no other way to start than, well, to begin. Take the first step of the journey. Put something, anything, on the page. Some writers enjoy listening to music while others prefer absolute silence. Nearly all prefer a window and a view.

Most students in class or at home will be unable to gaze out in tranquil contemplation upon an inspiring vista of natural beauty, but we can still maintain a quiet classroom environment for them to begin writing. If they are fortunate enough, students will have an appropriate place to work like a bedroom or the library—any environment suitable for this most arduous phase of the writing process, the first draft.

For many young people, first draft is synonymous with final draft. Teachers feel lucky if students read once over their papers to check for typos before turning it in. At its worst revising is tedious and Sisyphean, adjusting here, there, everywhere ad nauseam. But editing can also be eminently enjoyable, a potential source of true gratification.

Much like a painting comes into focus or a sculpture takes shape, a revised essay will start to tighten and flow. It may even begin to sing. At this stage writers will spend hours scrubbing, tweaking, and buffing, lost in an endless moment. As Irish playwright Oscar Wilde is attributed to have said, "I spent all morning putting in a comma, and all afternoon taking it away." It's true students may not have this luxury given the exigencies of a full class load, but the revision process has the potential to elevate the quality of an essay and may even prove surprisingly pleasurable to the young writer.

Students are often shocked to learn that books undergo scores of edits from multiple humans before publication. If this is unreasonable for an end-of-unit assessment, students should know the more they revise, the better their papers will be. In-class essays feature a condensed version of the same: think before beginning to write, create a game plan, jot down a simple structure, then let loose, saving a few minutes to read everything over before turning it in.

In the end students should understand there is much more to writing than completing an initial draft. It's imperative to brainstorm and outline before sitting down to address the blank page, and much joy can be found in polishing one's words and watching them begin to shine.

II. THE THESIS

There are as many different approaches to writing a thesis as there are to teaching a lesson. But what they all have in common is the notion that a thesis is what a piece of writing attempts to prove. If English teachers speak of a controlling idea, in social studies a thesis is about making a claim and backing it up. And for that matter what *is* the difference between a claim, an argument, and a thesis? Semantics and convention, largely. The truth is all three words can mean similar things to different people—and different things to similar people—and that's probably not going to change.

So as a way of cutting through the dissonance, consider this concrete formula to help students understand how to write a thesis:

Thesis = (counter argument) + claim + rationale.

For example: Although my sister prefers punk rock, reggae is the best genre of music because it is soulful, mellow, and melodic. (Remember content-free examples can be equally illustrative when teaching an aspect of writing.) Or: While the Luddites are sometimes viewed as anachronistic, their warnings about the dangers of new technology are relevant today due to increasing wealth inequality and the pressures of globalization.

Let's take each third of the thesis equation in turn. The counterargument is included in parentheses because it isn't always necessary. Some issues have two clearly defined sides so staking a claim in the affirmative—that the U.S.'s use of atomic weapons was legitimate, for example—immediately conjures the negative position that the 1945 bombings of Hiroshima and Nagasaki were unjust. In other instances, however, like an argument about the primary effects of European imperialism on Polynesian culture, a counterargument may be less obvious and therefore less necessary to include.

If there is one dispositively essential element of the thesis, it is the claim. Which is to say the main assertion of the work. Reggae is the best genre of music. The Luddites' warnings about the dangers of new technology are relevant today. The claim is the lynchpin of the thesis, its heart and driving force.

While the counterargument hinges on the claim, the rationale substantiates it. Why is reggae the best music? Because it's soulful, mellow, and melodic. Why are the Luddites' warnings about the dangers of new technology relevant today? Because of increasing wealth inequality and the pressures of globalization. A thesis's rationale are the reasons why a claim is true; they are the subarguments that will be corroborated with evidence and analysis throughout the essay.

Before moving on, it's worth mentioning a few additional points about the rationale in particular and theses in general. Some students feel the rationale is redundant because that's *literally* (as they would say) what the paper is about. And it's true this slippery slope argument holds some water. Why stop at the rationale? A student might ask. Why not continue to provide a rationale for the rationale? Why is reggae melodic? Because of the relative proximity of the notes. Why are the notes in proximity? And so on to the point of absurdity.

The purpose of a thesis is to lay out the controlling idea of a work, to give the reader a sense of what's coming and what you'll be attempting to prove. Just a claim (with the potential addition of a counterargument) is fine but adding a rationale, including a bit of the why, not only gives the reader something to chew on, it also provides clarity and a roadmap for what's to come. Like Goldilocks and her ursine porridge, a thesis should provide just the right amount of information for the reader. It should signal a direction. It should be clear, meaningful, and precise.

When students struggle, encourage them to talk it out. Ask students to tell you what they're trying to say, what's the main point they wish to prove. Students will often verbalize an excellent thesis without realizing their accomplishment. That's it! Write that down! you'll tell them with satisfaction.

This equation—(counterargument) + claim + rational—is admittedly but one approach to teaching students how to write a thesis. Theses can look quite different across various disciplines and genres. Some theses come at the beginning of a work and some arrive at the end. Some enthymematic essays may not even contain an explicit premise at all. The thesis equation is merely one way, albeit an exemplary one, of helping students craft controlling ideas with sufficient clarity and precision.

To sum up, while some believe a specific structure is unnecessary, it's important to teach students to write a thesis with a counterargument, claim, and rationale in order to admit competing points of view, clearly stake out a position, and provide a roadmap for the direction the forthcoming reasoning will take.

III. ANALYTICAL ESSAYS

At this point the heavy lifting is done. The full-length essay is teed up. The sports allusions have nearly run their course. Now that students understand how to write summaries and analytical paragraphs, know the difference between arguments, evidence, and analysis and can appreciate a well-crafted thesis, they are ready to tackle the analytical essay.

When explaining the nature of an essay to students, it's sometimes helpful to consider its etymology. "Essay" derives from the French verb *essayer*, which means to try. The sixteenth-century writer Michel de Montaigne is considered by many the father of the modern essay, in which he "attempts" to explore or convey an idea. At its most elemental that's all students are doing. They're unspooling a thought and seeing where it leads, hopefully tying it together at the conclusion or somewhere along the way.

Another more straightforward way to explain an essay is a piece of writing with a beginning, middle, and end. An analytical essay begins with an idea which is proven over the course of a number of paragraphs. Students should know that in addition to grabbing one's attention, the introduction to an analytical essay provides context, orienting the reader to the subject at hand, and usually ends with a thesis. The first body paragraphs may provide additional context or address an opposing point of view while the rest of the paper is devoted to substantiating the claim.

Since students will have had ample practice writing analytical paragraphs, they should be able to stack them sequentially like blocks, forming the architecture of an essay. And if students have written an instructive thesis, what they are going to say is already mapped out neatly in front of them. Students will mention the counterarguments before dismissing them in favor of their central claim, which they will then prove through the various rationales in subsequent analytical body paragraphs.

In an essay's conclusion, students will bind together their various strands of thought. They should revisit their thesis, summing up the main arguments and potentially the key evidence. Effective conclusions will also raise new questions, point to issues yet to be considered, and offer the reader some ideas about where they might go next. In this way students' essays will take their rightful place in the grand conversation of human knowledge, the crowd-sourced dialectic of all that has ever been known. (How's that for encouraging students to write?)

Like a good conclusion let's wrap up this chapter with some loose ends of our own. Analytical essays can be written either in class or at home with only minor changes in process between them. Each should involve some manner of prewriting, the latter more premeditated than the former.

With both in-class and take-home essays, the anatomy is the same: argument, evidence, analysis. One will develop over a longer period of time and therefore demand more care and attention, more polishing of words and ideas. The other will emerge in a brief spasm of thought and fade just as quick. If the take-home essay is your baby, the in-class essay is a shooting star.

And finally, the dilemma of the five-paragraph essay. Intro, three body paragraphs, conclusion. In many social studies departments the merits of the five-paragraph essay are hotly contested. This issue is a red herring, however, because the exact number of paragraphs in an analytical essay ultimately matters very little. Simply avoid the controversy. Eschew the antagonism. Give students an approximate word requirement and allow them to divide their sentences into paragraphs as they see fit, keeping in mind an essay's function and purpose.

The five-paragraph essay template can be a helpful scaffolding, yet it also has the potential to constrict emerging writers just beginning to come into their own. But with the right context students will learn to see an analytical essay as simply a vehicle for introducing and then proving an argument. An attempt at conveying an idea. No matter the number of paragraphs it takes them along the way.

If students are given the opportunity to practice writing analytical essays each unit, about once every four to six weeks, and if they receive regular feedback from their teacher and their peers, they will grow comfortable with the form and more confident in their ability to communicate. And ultimately, they'll become much better writers. An essential goal for social studies teachers one and all.

KEY IDEAS

- The constituent steps in the writing process are brainstorm, outline, write a first draft, revise, and polish.
- A social studies thesis should be clear, meaningful, and precise; and one way of teaching students how to write a thesis is with the equation thesis = (counterargument) + claim + rationale.
- Analytical essays are an extension of students' knowledge of analytical paragraphs and should be viewed as a way of proving a thesis through argument, evidence, and analysis.

THE WRITING PROCESS

Sometimes writing happens all at once in a burst of creative energy. Other times it is the product of a deliberate series of actions. For those moments when you are not hit with a thunderbolt of inspiration—and perhaps even when you are—it's important to be mindful of the stages in the writing process. They are *brainstorm, outline, write a first draft, revise,* and *polish.*

Use this handout as a checklist (and check-in) to make sure you are not skipping any steps. Consider marking off each as you go.

Assignment Prompt: _____
_____
_____
_____
_____
_____
_____

Writing Process Checklist

• Brainstorm completed
• Outline completed
• First draft completed
• Revisions completed
• Final polish completed

Since we have some room, and some time, use the remaining space to brainstorm. Write down words, sentences, bullets, scribbles, sketches, pictures, whatever comes to mind. The point is to begin generating ideas, a few of which you might actually use.

_____
_____
_____
_____
_____
_____
_____
_____
_____

Name
Date
Period

Title (Should be engaging)

Subtitle (Should be italicized and more specific than the title)

  I. Intro
    a. Hook
    b. Thesis
 II. Topic sentence or summary sentence of first body paragraph
    a. Key Evidence
    b. Key Evidence
III. Topic sentence or summary sentence of second body paragraph
    a. Key Evidence
    b. Key Evidence
    c. Key Evidence
IV. Add as many more body paragraphs as you need
 V. Conclusion
    a. Summary sentence
    b. Remaining issues, next steps, where to go from here

How to Write a Thesis

There are as many ways to write a thesis as there are students in a classroom. But what they all have in common is this: the thesis is the main idea your paper attempts to prove. It should be clear, meaningful, and precise. Here is a simple, concrete formula:

Thesis = (counterargument) + claim + rationale.

Keep in mind that the counterargument is in parentheses because it's not always necessary; the counterargument addresses any opposition to your thesis; the claim is your main assertion; the claim is the lynchpin and driving force of your thesis; the rationale substantiates your claim; the rationale are the reasons why your claim is true; the rationale are subarguments that will be corroborated with evidence and analysis.

Consider these thesis examples.

1. Although my sister prefers punk rock, reggae is the best genre of music because it is soulful, mellow, and melodic.
2. While the Luddites are sometimes viewed as anachronistic, their warnings about the dangers of new technology are relevant today due to increasing wealth inequality and the pressures of globalization.

Pro Tip: Words that signal your counterargument include *while, although, though, whereas, despite.* Words that signal your rationale include *because, since, as, then.*

Finally, a note about terminology. You may have heard other teachers refer to a thesis as the claim or argument. They're not wrong. Different people use these related words in different ways. Remember, most importantly, that your thesis is *the main point your paper is trying to prove.*

How to Write an Analytical Essay

Trivia time! Do you know where the word "essay" comes from? Hint: You may be studying this language in school. No, it's not the Spanish *ensayo*. "Essay" derives from the French verb *essayer*, which means to "try." The sixteenth-century writer Michel de Montaigne is considered by many the father of the modern essay, in which he "attempts" to explore or convey an idea. At its most elemental that's all you will be doing.

A more straightforward way to explain an essay is a piece of writing with a beginning, middle, and end. An analytical essay begins with an idea which you will prove over the course of a number of paragraphs. Here are a few tips: The introduction provides context, orients the reader to the subject at hand, and usually ends with a thesis; the thesis provides a great roadmap for the rest of the essay; the first body paragraphs can provide additional context or address an opposing point of view; the rest of the paper is devoted to proving your thesis; stack analytical paragraphs together to form the body of your essay; the conclusion should revisit the thesis, sum up the main arguments, and maybe even the key evidence; effective conclusions might also raise new questions, point to issues yet to be considered, and offer the reader some ideas about where to go next.

What about the classic five-paragraph essay format? Don't worry about it. Just remember to introduce your idea and take as many analytical body paragraphs as you need to prove it beyond a reasonable doubt. Then wrap up with a conclusion.

Finally, though analytical essays may seem daunting, they really aren't that bad. They can even be kind of fun. All you're doing is sharing your opinion and trying to back it up. Most of the time there's not even a right answer. Just defend your position as best you can. And remember that like its etymological cousin *essayer*, an essay is all about the "try."

Chapter 5

Academic Writing Part II

Research inspires curiosity, helps you break out of claustrophobic self-absorption and come to understand that you are not the only one who has passed down this road.

—*To Show and To Tell*, Phillip Lopate

I. DOCUMENT-BASED QUESTIONS

One specific genre of in-class essay is the DBQ, the document-based question. Mere mention of the acronym is enough to induce some students to cold sweats or keep them home from school with a dubious Ferris Bueller-inspired malady. But if students are already comfortable writing analytical essays, with the proper context and framing, the DBQ should not feel daunting at all.

Quite simply, students are given a prompt—usually in the form of a question—and then instructed to answer it using a variety of documents provided by the teacher. Hence "document-based" question. For example, What were the primary causes of the Russian Revolution? How are the democracies of Greece and Rome similar and how are they different? To what extent did the Homestead Acts contribute to the Dust Bowl?

The precise number of documents will vary depending on the nature of the assignment, the timing in the curriculum, and students' overall ability level. It might range from one to as many as ten and potentially even more. Documents can be images like photographs or political cartoons, passages like speeches or newspaper cuttings, or graphics like charts and tables.

The DBQ is an especially rigorous version of the analytical essay because it requires students to synthesize their ability to read and write and to apply discrete skills they've learned over the course of the semester. To begin, after making a mental note of the question at hand, students will need to classify and sort all documents using reading strategies like annotating and notetaking as well as their powers of analysis. Let's say students are tasked with making sense of eight documents concerning the causes of the Russian Revolution (or revolutions plural, to be precise). They receive the documents in this order:

A) Quote from Tsar Nicholas II
B) Political cartoon from a Russian newspaper
C) Pyramid caricature of Russian social classes
D) Chart of Russian inequality prior to the revolution
E) Photograph of the Berlin Wall
F) Painting of Bloody Sunday
G) Newspaper editorial about the Haitian Revolution
H) Excerpt from the memoirs of Alexander Kerensky

Students will have to read over each document to determine how it does (or does not) help answer the question. Marking up the documents directly, through highlighting, underlining, or writing in the margins, is particularly efficient. After all documents are correctly classified, they should be sorted into groups or buckets. Students will then formulate a list which might look something like this:

Political cause: A and H.
Social cause: B and C.
Economic cause: D and F.
Don't need: E and G.

Organizing the documents in this way is an initial stage of prewriting. They've digested a deluge of information, categorized it, and now students must put it to use. The puzzle pieces are beginning to come together. What are the primary causes of the Russian Revolution? Well, what answer to that question do the documents support? Write that answer and—presto!—you have your thesis.

The primary causes of the Russian Revolution were political, social, and economic. Or *An oppressive government and the inequalities of serfdom were the main causes of the Russian Revolution.* (Note both theses have neither a counterargument nor rationale, only a claim.) And what about the catastrophe of WWI? Since the documents avoid mentioning it, the war will be difficult to use as evidence.

Even though the DBQ is likely an in-class essay, students should still take time to prewrite. Briefly jotting down their thesis and a list of sorted documents creates a perfectly workable outline, especially given the constraints of the assignment.

At this stage the essay becomes like any other. Students will support their thesis with evidence and analysis in the form of analytical body paragraphs, an exercise in which they'll already be well practiced. The only extra wrinkle is citing their various documents explicitly throughout the essay. *Document F, which shows the military firing on protestors at the Winter Palace, clearly illustrates government oppression was a key cause of the revolution.*

Timed writing is by nature a hurried—and harried—experience. It lacks the cautious consideration of a process piece. Nonetheless, when students have finished, they should take several minutes to review their work and proofread or if needed revise. The whole ordeal will be over before they know it. As with so much in life, anticipation is frequently worse than the dreaded event itself.

When framed as merely an extension of the analytical essay, which itself is but an expansion of the analytical paragraph, the DBQ is more likely to be viewed by students as doable—as an opportunity to show what they've learned rather than scurry to the bathroom or call in sick with clammy hands and a fevered brow.

Students! Fear not the DBQ. Writing is your sword and your shield, and a salve for the most virulent of academic afflictions.

II. THE RESEARCH PAPER

For some reason students are initially less overwhelmed by the research paper than they are by a DBQ despite the fact that the former is exceedingly more intricate. Perhaps this is because DBQs happen all at once whereas the research paper is constructed over a matter of months. One cannot see the forest for the trees and gets lost, often blissfully, meandering from guidepost to guidepost. While in some ways a research paper is easier than a DBQ, it's also more involved and requires a host of additional skills.

The research paper is also the apotheosis of academic writing. It's a challenge students should undertake in each class, each year. Like the DBQ the research paper is really just an augmentation of the analytical essay—but with the added requirement that students cite their sources. It's also a process paper, which means students' final drafts should be buffed to a high sheen. Tell students that though a months-long research paper sounds forbidding, you'll walk with them every step of the way, teach them every new skill to be learned, and before they know it they'll have a major piece of writing under their belts about which they can be proud.

The key phases of the research paper are as follows:

Select a topic, develop a research question, decide on a notetaking style, conduct research, review paraphrasing versus direct quotes, review source evaluation techniques, craft a thesis, make an outline, review citation methods, write the first draft, edit and revise, produce a final copy.

The steps are many, which means scaffolding the process for students is critically important, even if sooner or later they'll need to internalize it on their own.

The first and in some ways most important decision for students is topic selection. Teachers can assign topics for students or general subjects like the Holocaust or the New Deal, but the research paper is a great opportunity for student choice. So cast a wide net, allowing students to choose any subject they'd like as long as it relates to the course curriculum.

In U.S. History, for example, set two criteria: the subject must involve America and it must be historical. That's it. Encourage students to find an issue in which they're interested if not passionate. Perhaps this is a person, movement, conflict, or event they'd like to learn more about, someone who sparks their interest or something they'd like to explore in greater detail. The point is if students are interested in their topic, they'll ultimately be more successful. After all when work is pleasurable, it ceases to be work. This is as true of research papers as it is of a career, even life. Topic selection may seem like a minor step, but the effects are consequential.

Once students have an idea about the subject or theme they'd like to investigate, they should develop a research question. Its purpose is to frame student thinking, eventually culminating in an answer that will serve as the paper's thesis. Questions beginning with "how" and "why" tend to be more effective than those beginning with "what" because they require more analytical and less descriptive answers. Questions focusing on evaluation or causes or effects are often best, though compare-contrast questions are illustrative as well.

Why did the United States belatedly become involved in WWI? How did the excesses of the Gilded Age lead to the reforms of the Progressive Era? The first question is about causes and the second effects. What are the origins of the California minimum wage? What were the main consequences of the 1840s Irish Potato Famine? These questions indicate cause and effect respectively even though both begin with "what."

Was John Muir an American hero? Were the tactics of Malcolm X or Martin Luther King Jr. more effective? These evaluative questions begin without a "what," "why," or "how" at all, yet they're still undeniably suitable subjects for student investigation.

Research questions should also be appropriate in scope. The history of Latin American colonialism is much too broad for one to examine over several months, while the price elasticity of supply during Mohandas Gandhi's Great Salt March of 1930 is clearly much too specific. Here again the Goldilocks rule reigns supreme: not too wide or too narrow but just right. Encourage students to winnow down their questions as much as possible, keeping in mind that truly original research is likely a bridge too far. Certainly the more specific the better but at some point uncovering sufficient research becomes prohibitively difficult to achieve.

To inspire students, consider inviting to your class a guest speaker like the school or local librarian or even a professional researcher working in the field of history, government, political science, geography, or economics. Students will enjoy seeing the transferability of these skills, and they may even be surprised to know some people get paid for doing the research they love.

When it's time to jump in, don't just tell kids to go research, of course. Teach them how. Give students the option of taking notes three different ways: the notecard method, the print-'em-out method, and the digital method. Notecards are quintessentially old school, but the occasional student prefers their simplicity and doesn't mind any inefficiencies in the process. One side of the card includes evidence and analysis and the other bibliographic information.

For students who don't want to handwrite every quote and paraphrase, the print-'em-out method let's students—you guessed it—print out articles and provide analysis via annotation directly on the sources themselves. Students can store stapled stacks of paper in a folder the same way notecards of yore were kept in a shoebox. Plus as an added benefit: the complete citation will already appear on the document for future use.

Though both print-'em-out and notecard variants are helpful for some students, most will naturally gravitate to the digital method. Show students how to create a table with two columns and limitless rows in an electronic document. Label the left column Source and the right column Notes and pull the spine between both westward so the former is about one third of the later.

Students can simply type the title of the source in the first box, linking directly to it for future retrieval. In the box to the right students will paste limitless evidence without fear of plagiarism. One space below they'll write analysis as needed, explaining how the evidence relates to their research question. This method is efficient but the tendency toward disorganization is high, and the lure of convenience may sabotage the thoughtless student.

If someone dislikes these three options—and one or two students always will—tell them to propose their own research notetaking style provided it includes several essential criteria. Regardless of the format all notes should include complete source citation information, a way of distinguishing between paraphrased and directly quoted evidence, and some form of analysis.

Citation info is vital since students will need to reference all words and ideas that are not their own. Understanding the difference between a direct quote and a paraphrase is important because students should know if they're crediting someone else for their words and ideas, or simply their ideas alone. And though in truth not every piece of evidence requires discrete analysis, it's helpful for students to comment on the information as they proceed so they'll remember how a source relates to their subject, theme, or research question when sitting down to write.

Hopefully at this point in the school year students will be well versed in the concepts of argument, evidence, and analysis, having already written a number of different essays and a plethora of paragraphs. If they don't know the difference between paraphrasing and quoting directly, now is a good time to teach them. The concepts are fairly straightforward: the former uses someone else's ideas but with altered phrasing while the later copies both words and ideas verbatim. Simply placing quotation marks around direct quotes in one's notes, no matter the style, is an easy way to differentiate.

As practice use the corresponding handout at the end of the chapter or create one yourself. Have students take several samples of evidence from their notes and turn them into paraphrases and direct quotes. (We'll discuss other skills like introducing evidence and citing it in text later in this chapter.)

If all this weren't enough, there are several additional considerations for students to keep in mind. One is source evaluation. Students should be reminded to consider the veracity of each document, to examine its provenance and not solely its utility. Ask them to recall the CRAAP test, the warning signs of a shady website, the critical thinking skills of a historian or economist. You might even task students with ranking the trustworthiness of their own sources on a scale of one to ten. Those six or lower consider omitting entirely.

Also, decide how many primary sources and—gasp—how many *physical* books you'll require in the final Works Cited. Demanding primary sources will nudge students toward genuine scholarship and discourage them from cutting corners, while books reinforce the often underappreciated notion that knowledge exists separate and apart from the internet. Ten total sources, three of which are primary and two of which are books, is a reasonable place to start.

Clearly this stage of the research paper, the research itself, is most time consuming. Students should have multiple hours to work in class over the course of a number of weeks, with the additional opportunity to finish at home as needed. And though you'll need to set a date by which students' research is complete, in truth the research is never finished. It merely stops when one runs out of time or, in the fortunate event, has enough information to begin. Students should also know the process is dynamic—they might begin writing, realize some aspect of the paper is light on citations and dive back in for more documentation or another quote.

Sooner or later the time will come to move from researching to writing. Connecting the two are the thesis and outline. The thesis, as you know, is the primary argument one attempts to substantiate over the course of the paper. If students have written their theme and research question at the top of their notes—which is a nice trick for funneling one's thoughts—they can at this point add their answer to the question, which is to say the thesis.

Give students a handout, like the one at the end of this chapter, for help in brainstorming and ultimately constructing a thesis. Remind them of the (counterargument) + claim + rationale formulation and that they need not be beholden to it. And if students struggle synthesizing their thoughts into a unitary sentence, offer to talk it through, encouraging them to speak conversationally until the words begin to flow. You might be surprised how often this tactic is successful.

Students who are floundering may also need to conduct more research. They must dig and dig before an answer to their question is revealed. Theses take a great deal of craftsmanship, and it's not unusual for such sentences to require thorough shaping before cohering into a final product. Once students have a sturdy thesis, the end is almost if not entirely in sight.

The real light at the end of the tunnel is the outline. Students need not map out each body paragraph but rather order and delineate their key ideas, as discussed in chapter 4. Outlines can assume many forms but, conceptually, should tie subarguments and essential evidence to the thesis like a marionette—each arm linking back to the larger claim. And if students follow the thesis formula, a roadmap for the outline should be apparent: after the introduction mention the counterargument before proving the paper's central claim, rationale by rationale.

Let's say, for example, that the thesis posits two main effects of gerrymandering. *While some claim gerrymandering is inevitable, it is negatively affecting American politics through increased polarization and decreased electoral competition.* This outline, like the paper itself, will briefly consider the purported inevitability of gerrymandering, then move to the negative effects of increased polarization and the negative effects of decreased electoral competitiveness, recapitulating as necessary in the conclusion. The number of particular paragraphs for each is immaterial, provided there exists a logical organization of ideas.

For some writers this may be enough. But adding at least the most important evidence under each rationale will enable students to see if they indeed have adequate research to support each point they are attempting to prove.

If they're unable to produce the evidence they'll either need to continue researching or alter their argument to align with the information they've acquired. Two to three pieces of evidence for each subargument should suffice.

When students have a working outline supported by plenty of research, they will want to start writing. Or at least they will recognize some unknowable urge to begin, alongside an equally unknowable desire to procrastinate. But how to write a research paper? How is this genre different from other essays? The answer, of course, lies in the citations. Students must give credit for others' words and ideas, for the research they will be including in support of their own opinions. This notion is as simple to understand as it is difficult to execute.

There are two aspects of citing sources in a research paper—in-text citations and the Works Cited—and one cannot function without the other. The Works Cited is the complete alphabetized list of sources with all necessary bibliographic information: author, title, year, publisher, etcetera. A sizeable number of students will think a Works Cited is the beginning and end of a research paper's citation requirements but, lo, they will be disappointed.

Creating a Works Cited is a relatively straightforward endeavor. Especially with the advent of online sites like Easy Bib, which automatically generate a bibliographic citation with as little as a web address. The challenge and the art of the research paper, however, lies in its in-text citations. As the name would suggest, these citations occur in the corpus of the paper itself rather than as a coda at the end. The reader must be made aware of any words and ideas, direct quotes and paraphrases, that do not originate with the writer. And a Works Cited on its own leaves no way for the reader to ascertain specifically what intellectual property belongs to whom.

Inserting abridged citations into the body of an essay solves this problem. The reader can make note of the in-text citation and, if desired, jump to the Works Cited page for a full description of its bibliographic content. In-text citations are shortened for the simple reason that reading over the full citation would be cumbersome and distracting in the extreme.

There are three main citation formats with which students should be familiar: MLA, Chicago, and APA. Each boasts its own detailed style manual available online and in print. Since entire books are devoted to their explication, let's simply overview the general design of all three.

MLA or Modern Language Association uses parenthetical in-text citations (students are sometimes interested to know parenthetical is the adjectival form of parenthesis). What specific information is found in the parenthetical citation can be tricky but as a general rule simply tell students to include whatever will be listed first in the Works Cited entry. If it's the author's last name, include that; if there is no explicit author list an abbreviated article title, and so on. One advantage of parenthetical citations is they are embedded in the syntax, allowing one's eyes to glide left to right rather than bounce up and down.

Chicago is the citation method most often used by historians. Based on the *Chicago Manual of Style* it features footnotes as in-text citations with full or partial bibliographic information found at the bottom of the page, along with the corresponding footnote number, as well as in the Works Cited, which in Chicago style is called a Bibliography.

The Chicago method may also incorporate endnotes, which are like footnotes but found at the end of a writing rather than the bottom of each page. Interestingly if full citation information is included in footnotes a separate Bibliography is not officially required, though it makes sense to demand students incorporate one nonetheless.

If a drawback to Chicago is the extra work required of one's eyes while reading, an advantage is its simplicity. Often it's easier for students to apply numerically footnoted citations rather than decipher which information to include in parenthesis, where to include the parenthetical citation (sometimes in the middle of a sentence but more commonly at the end), and how to structure the citation grammatically (the period always follows the final closed parenthesis).

Finally APA, the acronym for American Psychological Association, is a style common to the social sciences. APA uses parenthetical in-text citations much like MLA with some slight variations involving page numbers, publication dates, commas, ampersands, and so on. The MLA Works Cited and Chicago Bibliography in APA is called a Reference.

APA style may have the broadest range for students and teachers because it spans so many of the social sciences. Given its resemblance to MLA, APA may be easier to learn for students who are already familiar with MLA from English classes. Of course, the opposite may also be true: students might get confused by their likeness, twisted around by the subtle differences. If working closely with an English teaching partner, you may want to adopt one style for clarity. Or you and your social studies department might decide that teaching all three styles will best prepare students for life after high school and the rigors of college.

Whether MLA, APA, or Chicago, you'll likely also want to teach students a few helpful tricks. When citing a source for the first time, for example, introduce it in a sentence rather than a footnote or parenthesis. "According to Harvard political scientist Theda Skocpol, who in *Social Revolutions in the Modern World*, writes." This setup provides necessary context, easing one into the source and making each subsequent in-text citation easier for the reader to digest.

If students wish to cite a long quotation, say more than four or five lines in length, they should indent the entirety of the passage, placing it in what is known as "block format." Specific citation requirements vary from MLA to APA to Chicago, but all three utilize indented block formatting to make comprehension easier for the reader.

Conversely, if students want to omit words from a quotation, they should use ellipses to signal to the reader they are cutting unnecessary verbiage. Shortening a direct quote is often useful for the reader and writer alike, and ellipses make the writer's intentions transparent.

Students should add their own words to a quotation for clarifying purposes only, and they should do so with brackets. Pronouns, archaic or technical prose, and obscure colloquialisms are examples of words and phrases that might benefit from being replaced.

Finally, a note about the politics of citations. Sometimes in life one has to play the game, and citing sources is no exception. This may be worth mentioning to students. The more citations the more professional an academic research paper will read, and thus the better chance it will have of getting published or earning an exemplary grade. So sprinkle as many sources as possible throughout your essay. Jump through the necessary hoops. This will not be the last time in life you'll feel compelled to do the same.

Whichever citation method students chose they are wise to remember the big picture. They should understand the rationale for citing sources and the relationship between in- and end-of-text citations. They should not fear being accused of plagiarism for misplacing an errant period or excluding a footnote. Instead, they should be given multiple opportunities to master these difficult skills and to appreciate that giving credit for another's words and ideas is the right thing to do, the very foundation of academic advancement and the pursuit of knowledge.

Once students have learned how to credit sources, they should plow headlong into the first draft. As mentioned in chapter 4, this is a perilous stage of the journey—yet there is no choice except to begin. With a detailed roadmap, students should feel confident about the direction their argument will take and the evidence they will use to get there. They have their notes and a thesis-driven outline and now they must turn both into an essay. This will take some students hours, some days, some even weeks. But no matter the length of time, finishing a draft is like reaching the summit of a mountain: it's all downhill from there.

Hopefully, students have received feedback at every step along the way, from selecting a topic and developing a research question to taking notes, generating a thesis, and crafting an outline. The first draft is no exception. Mandating that students' papers undergo at least one peer edit is an effective—and efficient—means of revision. Since the draft will undoubtedly require countless changes, use a peer editing handout like the one included at the end of this chapter to communicate your many suggestions indirectly.

For example, did you mention the importance of an engaging title and informative subtitle? If not, students will know this is imperative after receiving peer feedback via the worksheet. You might also allow students the choice of editing their partner's paper electronically or on the hard copy itself. Once the edit is complete, have students deliver the feedback orally. Ask them to list two positive aspects of the draft and two aspects that could be improved, though they'll probably have much more to say.

For teachers, giving formative feedback on a process paper is a noble feat. To assess a paper twice is extraordinary, thrice heroic. After informal check-ins during the early stages and a quick glance to ensure students have at least completed some semblance of a draft, you may feel you've done enough. For students who'd like individualized help, you might offer meeting at other available times throughout the week or your particular school day. For some teachers this will be plenty. For those willing to collect a process paper multiple times, you deserve an award. And a trophy. And a ribbon.

At the very least ensure students do not equate first draft with final draft. Some undoubtedly will so emphasize the importance of edits and revisions. Do their words flow into sentences and their sentences into paragraphs? How clear are their controlling ideas, how persuasive their arguments as a whole? Mention that refining one's work is immensely rewarding, at times even joyful. Explain it's fun discovering just how good one's writing can become.

Sooner or later you'll have to set a due date. Remind students of the proper heading—name, date, period, etcetera—and the way in which you'd like their work submitted, and consider using a digital plagiarism detector as well. No cover pages or baroque brass brad-fastened folders, please. Distribute a final paper checklist, essentially a reworking of the peer editing handout, so students make extra certain they're not misplacing or leaving anything out.

From start to finish the process will take several months, perhaps weeks if that's all you're doing in class. It won't be easy, but students should feel proud of their accomplishment and more confident in their ability to research and cite sources effectively. They should know such papers will surely be required of them at higher levels of academia, maybe even their future professions.

At long last, students have climbed the mountain and descended to safety. They have completed their journey, accomplishing a feat many would not have thought possible at the outset or various points along the way. Yet in the end they have persevered, and now they are done.

KEY IDEAS

- A document-based question (DBQ) is a version on an analytical essay in which students are required to reference specific documents in support of their thesis.
- Key to a successful DBQ is answering the question directly, classifying and sorting the documents, and including them in one's outline and essay explicitly.
- The essential elements of a research paper are select a topic, develop a research question, decide on a notetaking style, conduct research, review paraphrasing versus direct quotes, review source evaluation techniques, craft a thesis, make an outline, review citation methods, write the first draft, edit and revise, produce a final copy.
- The research paper is the apogee of academic writing and a challenge students should face in each class, every year.

How to Write a Document-Based Question Essay

Students, fear not the DBQ. This type of essay is merely an extension of the analytical essays you already know how to write. The only difference is you will be provided with the documents, the evidence, with which you'll answer a particular question. That's it. Consider these questions: What were the primary causes of the Russian Revolution? How are the democracies of Greece and Rome similar and how are they different? To what extent did the Homestead Acts contribute to the Dust Bowl? Each question could be a DBQ.

Sometimes you'll receive one document, sometimes as many as ten. They can be images like photographs or political cartoons, passages like speeches or newspaper cuttings, or graphics like charts and tables. The documents will probably also be a combination of primary and secondary sources. Follow these steps to arrive at a successfully written DBQ: (1) Read the question! (2) Read all the documents (think about annotating them or taking a few notes). (3) Classify the documents*. (4) Sort the documents into groups**. (5) Brainstorm. (6) Outline. (7) Write the essay. (8) Revise and polish.

*Classify documents by labeling them as they relate to the question. For example, from the Russian Revolution question above, some documents might be social causes, some economic, and some political. **Once you've classified or categorized the documents, put them into groups (all the social causes together, all the economic causes together, etcetera).

Notice how after the fourth step a DBQ becomes just like any other in-class essay? Follow the regular writing process and ta-da—you're finished. One pro tip: Don't forget to cite the documents explicitly in your essay. "Document B illustrates that . . ." "Document D, on the other hand, shows. . ." And that's it! Easy stuff. You're now ready to tackle DBQs. Good luck!

How to Write a Research Paper

If content is temporary, skills last forever. Have you forgotten how to ride a bike? Can you still remember who assassinated the Hungarian Archduke Franz Ferdinand in 1914, setting in motion WWI? Exactly. You may forget things, but you're less likely to forget *how to do* things.

In many ways research paper writing is the culmination of your social studies writing skills. It involves not only writing persuasively, supporting an original argument with evidence and analysis, but also citing your sources, giving credit for others' words and ideas.

These are some of the skills involved in writing a research paper:

Reading; *notetaking*; *summarizing*; *thesis creation*; *paraphrasing*; *quoting*; *analyzing*; *citing sources.*

As you can see, there's a lot you need to be able to do.

And these are the key steps in writing a research paper:

Select a topic; *develop a research question*; *decide on a notetaking style*; *conduct research*; *learn or review paraphrasing versus direct quotes*; *learn or review source evaluation techniques*; *craft a thesis*; *make an outline*; *learn or review citation methods*; *write the first draft*; *edit and revise*; *produce a final copy.*

We will go over each step together so don't worry, agonize, or fret. The good news is you'll get to select your own topic (within the boundaries of the course). This is a great opportunity for you to learn more about a subject in which you're interested. Not sure what you're interested in? No problem— start researching and see what strikes your fancy!

Selecting a Research Paper Topic

Selecting a topic is perhaps the most important part of your entire research paper. It's also the easiest (except when it's the hardest). Remember you can choose any subject as long as it relates to the course curriculum. Try to find something you're passionate about. If you're not passionate about anything, settle for something in which you're interested. This might be a person, a movement, an issue, a conflict, an event, etcetera.

The more interested you are in your subject, the less your research will seem like work, and therefore the more successful you'll be. Topic selection may seem like a minor step but the effects are consequential indeed.

Use the space below to brainstorm. What are you passionate about? What are you interested in? What might you be interested in? What are you definitely not interested in? Get the cerebral juices flowing and jot down some initial thoughts and ideas.

_____
_____
_____
_____
_____
_____
_____
_____
_____
_____
_____
_____
_____
_____
_____
_____
_____
_____
_____
_____
_____
_____
_____
_____
_____
_____

Framing Your Research

What is the general theme of your research? This is the overall subject you are studying.

_____
_____
_____
_____
_____
_____
_____
_____

What is your research question? This is the question that will guide your research and that you will ultimately answer in your research paper. Questions starting with "why" and "how" are usually better than questions starting with "what" because they tend to call for less descriptive and more analytical or argumentative answers.

_____
_____
_____
_____
_____
_____
_____
_____
_____

What is your thesis? Your thesis is the answer to your research question. (Don't fill this out now because you haven't done any research and clearly don't yet know the answer.)

_____
_____
_____
_____
_____
_____
_____
_____
_____

How to Take Notes for Research

There are a number of different methods of taking notes on the research you are conducting. Whatever method you choose, however, must include several important things. They are: complete bibliographic information; a way to determine if you are paraphrasing or quoting directly; a plan for differentiating between evidence and your analysis.

Option #1 Digital Notes. You can use a computer to take notes on your research by making a table.

Source Information	Notes
Put all *bibliographic* info here. (You can do this with a hyperlink if you'd like.)	*Evidence*: This is the info you get from your source. It can be quoted directly or paraphrased, but make sure you can tell the difference. *Wording*: You may want to write exact or paraphrased here. Or you can use quotation marks above. *Analysis*: This is where you write something about the evidence. What is it? How does it relate to your thesis? How might you use it? That sort of stuff.

Option #2 Print 'Em Out. You can print your sources and annotate them. If using this method, your analysis will be written on the pages themselves. And the source information should already be included on the printout.

Option #3 Note Cards. You can take notes by hand on notecards. The evidence, wording, and analysis will go on the front of the card. The bibliographic or source information will go on the back.

Paraphrase Versus Direct Quote

Understanding the difference between a direct quote and a paraphrase is important because you should know if you're crediting someone else for their words and ideas, or simply their ideas alone. Here is a quick review: a paraphrase uses someone else's ideas but with altered phrasing in your own words; a direct quote copies another's words and ideas verbatim; paraphrases do not need "quotation marks" but direct quotes do.

Remember that your research notes and your research paper must both clearly distinguish between the two. If your paper does not, you may be guilty of the p-word.* Use evidence from your research notes to practice below. (Don't worry yet about citing these sources. We'll go over that shortly.)

1. Write a direct quote.

2. Paraphrase the above quote.

3. Write another direct quote.

4. Paraphrase the above quote.

*Which is plagiarism, but don't be scared. There's a big difference between accidentally messing up a paraphrase and deliberately copying someone else's essay. The former is understandable, but the latter is pretty messed up.

Source Evaluation for a Research Paper

Remember that differentiating *between* sources is as important as finding them.

What are the most important things to keep in mind when determining if a source is legitimate?

_____

_____

_____

_____

_____

_____

List the full citation information below for three of your sources and then evaluate their trustworthiness. Circle a number from 1 to 10 (10 is best, 1 worst) and explain your answer.

Source #1   1   2   3   4   5   6   7   8   9   10

_____

_____

_____

_____

_____

_____

Source #2   1   2   3   4   5   6   7   8   9   10

_____

_____

_____

_____

_____

Source #3   1   2   3   4   5   6   7   8   9   10

_____

_____

_____

_____

_____

Research Paper Source Requirements

For your research paper you will need at least ten sources, three of which must be primary sources and one of which must be a physical book. Your research paper will have a Works Cited page, also known as a Bibliography, as well as in-text citations. Other than these specific source requirements, how much evidence do you need? How many notes must you take? The real answer, though more vague and less specific, is *enough to convincingly prove your thesis.*

If you'd like, you can use this handout as a tool to monitor your source totals.

1. [Book Source]

2. [Primary Source]

3. [Primary Source]

4. [Primary Source]

5. [Secondary Source]

6. [Secondary Source]

7. [Secondary Source]

8. [Secondary Source]

9. [Secondary Source]

10. [Secondary Source]

Research Pro Tips

Below is advice for stepping up your research game. Research like a pro!

Google: (1) If you end your search with site:.edu, then only websites ending in .edu will show up. Example: Weimar political economy site:.edu. (You can do site-colon-dot anything, by the way, and you'll only get those results. Like site:.org or site:.gov or site:.com.) (2) Use Google's Advanced Search. Just google "advanced search" and use the Advanced Search page to narrow and refine your results. (3) To find words in their exact order, put quotes around them. Otherwise your search will find pages with those words included but not one after the other. For example: "origins of totalitarianism in Russia."

Quickly Scan for Key Words: (1) Use Ctrl F to find key words you're looking for on a page. If you encounter a lengthy reading and try to skim for key words, but get tired slogging through all the unnecessary information, just press Ctrl and F at the same time, then type your word(s) in the search box that appears. All those words will then be highlighted in the text.

Library Databases: (1) Go to your school's library website and consult the various databases. There are many to choose from, and several that are specifically for social studies. What is the huge benefit of these databases? You are assured that all the information is legit and citable. (2) Side note: If you can, try Jstor. It's a premier digital library often used in college and graduate school. But it usually requires a paid subscription.

Books: (1) Books are like mini search engines and databases refined, printed out, and rolled—or pressed!—into one. Consult a library to find these one-of-a-kind objects.

How to Write a Thesis for Your Research Paper

A thesis is the main idea of your paper. It's what you are trying to substantiate or prove. The thesis should be meaningful, clear, and precise. Here's a simple equation to better understand its key parts: *thesis = counterargument + claim + rationale*. Example: While cheeseburgers are delicious, carne asada burritos are the world's best food because of their marinated meat, tangy salsas, and efficient handling.

Counterargument: This is a nod to those who may disagree with you ("While cheeseburgers are delicious"). You don't always have to include a counterargument but it can make your thesis more sophisticated and advanced. Words that signal your counterargument include *while*, *although*, *though*, *whereas*, *despite*.

Claim: This is the big or main idea of your paper ("carne asada burritos are the world's best food"). It should clearly stake out a position (or "steak" out a position, as it were).

Rationale: This is the justification of your claim ("because of their marinated meat, tangy salsas, and efficient handling"). The rationale often includes several parts or reasons; the classic formulation is three but you need not limit yourself to this number. Words that signal your rationale include *because, since, then, as*.

Finally, the cool thing about this thesis formulation is it creates a nice outline for your paper. After your introduction, which ends with your thesis, discuss your counterargument, then your different rationale, then conclude with a conclusion and you're finished!

But don't get bogged down with these details. Remember that at its core a thesis is just the main idea of your paper. That's it. This is just one way of writing a good thesis. There are many more.

A Guide to In-Text Citations

You probably know what a Bibliography or Works Cited is. But did you also know you need to cite your sources in the body of your essay as well? These are called "in-text" citations, and they're necessary because the reader must be made aware of any words and ideas that do not originate with the writer. And a Works Cited on its own leaves no way for the reader to ascertain specifically what belongs to whom. Inserting shortened citations into the body of your paper solves this problem. (In-text citations are shortened for the simple reason that reading over the full citation would be cumbersome and distracting.) There are three main citation formats to be aware of: MLA, Chicago, and APA. Since each has its own detailed style manual available online and in books, let's just go over them briefly.

MLA: MLA is an acronym for Modern Language Association. It uses "parenthetical" in-text citations. For example, (Coates 117). One advantage of parenthetical citations is they are embedded in the syntax, allowing one's eyes to glide left to right rather than bounce up and down.

Chicago: Chicago is the citation method most often used by historians. It's based on the *Chicago Manual of Style* and features footnotes as in-text citations. If a drawback to Chicago is the extra work required of one's eyes while reading, an advantage is its simplicity. Footnotes can be easier to learn than parenthetical citations.

APA: APA is an acronym for the American Psychological Association. Common in the social sciences, APA uses parenthetical in-text citations much like MLA with some slight variations involving page numbers, publication dates, commas, etcetera. Fun fact: the MLA Works Cited and Chicago Bibliography in APA is called a Reference.

First Draft Peer Editing

Provide detailed, thoughtful feedback on each of the following. Remember the Golden Rule.

1. Is there an engaging title and informative subtitle? How can each be improved?

2. Are the first several sentences a sufficiently engaging hook? How can the hook be improved?

3. Does the next part of the introduction provide helpful context? Does it orient the reader to the topic?

4. Is the thesis the last line of the introduction? Does it need a beginning like "This paper will argue?" Is the thesis specific and argumentative? Does it have a counterargument, claim, and rationale? Does the thesis provide a roadmap or a structure for the rest of the paper? Can it be improved?

5. Is the first paragraph of the body a background paragraph? Does it need to be?

6. Does each body paragraph have a topic sentence relating directly to the thesis? Mark all that don't. Does each topic sentence include a transition? If not, mark each sentence that needs one.

7. Does each body paragraph have enough evidence? Mark all that need more. Is all evidence properly cited? Mark each place a citation is missing or incorrect. (This is very important!) Does each body paragraph have enough analysis, tying evidence to the thesis? Mark all that need more.

8. Are the main points sufficiently restated in the conclusion? Are the key ideas extended to consider remaining questions, further research, what to do next? How might the conclusion be improved?

9. Does the Works Cited follow the proper format? How can it be improved?

10. Are there at least ten sources? Are three of the ten primary sources? Is one an actual book?

11. List at least three things that are really good about your partner's paper!

Research Paper Final Draft Checklist

Make sure your final draft is consistent with the guidelines below.

Formatting: Is your name, date, and class period double-spaced in the upper left-hand corner? Is there an engaging title and informative subtitle one space below? Is your paper at least 1,500 words in length and double-spaced in the right font?

Citation: Is each piece of evidence properly cited in-text? Is the Works Cited correct and included at the end of the final draft? Are there at least ten sources, three of which are primary sources and one of which is a book?

Introduction: Are the first several sentences a sufficiently engaging hook? Does the next part of the introduction provide helpful context? Is the last line of the introduction the thesis? Is the thesis specific and argumentative? Does the thesis provide a roadmap or a structure for the rest of the paper?

Body: Is the first paragraph of the body a background paragraph? Does it need to be? Does each body paragraph have an effective, argumentative topic sentence? Does each topic sentence include a transition? Is there enough evidence to prove your thesis? Is all evidence properly cited? Does each body paragraph include sufficient analysis?

Conclusion: Are the main points sufficiently restated? Are the main ideas extended to consider remaining questions, further research, what to do next?

Miscellaneous: *Do not* include a title page. *Do not* put your paper in a folder or sleeve.

Chapter 6

Real-World Writing

Ultimately every writer must follow the path that feels most comfortable. For most people learning to write, that path is nonfiction. It enables them to write about what they know or can observe or can find out. This is especially true of young people and students. They will write far more willingly about subjects that touch their own lives or that they have an aptitude for. Motivation is at the heart of writing.

—*On Writing Well*, William Zinsser

I. LONG LIVE NONFICTION

Outside traditional academic writing like research papers and in-class essays lies a universe of nonfiction, one with which students may be wholly unfamiliar. Many students might be surprised to learn that each year considerably more nonfiction than fiction books are published with consistently higher sales and greater profitability, yet for some reason they still associate writing with English rather than social studies. While nonfiction is part and parcel of English curricula, it should be equally integral to our disciplines as well.

Perhaps the best way of achieving this goal is to show students the wide range of writing that exists beyond the bounds of the typical classroom assignment. Students will undoubtedly be able to apply analytical essay skills to their studies and careers down the road, but why not create opportunities to practice the types of writing they encounter in their lives today? Real-world writing is by definition more authentic, allowing for better assessments and—since students are likely to be more highly motivated—better writing too. This is the true goal of our work.

Indeed it is difficult to imagine a type of nonfiction that cannot be adapted for classroom use. For that matter even fiction, like historical fiction, makes for engaging student work. Consider the writing one encounters in society: *Op-eds, book reviews, magazine features, white papers, legal briefs, family histories, memoirs, speeches, visual essays,* and *comics.* Surely there are many more, all begging to join their more-traditional academic friends.

What follows, then, is a compendium of assignments. Try one or try them all. After thinking about teaching writing in this way—as mirroring what is actually produced outside the confines of a school—you'll undoubtedly dream up other ideas of your own. Enjoy experimenting with the limitless variations of real-world social studies writing.

II. OP-ED

Op-ed is short for "opposite editorial," which denotes its location in a newspaper or magazine. Some students believe op-ed means "opinion-editorial" and they are also correct. An op-ed is an opinion essay—it just technically adheres to a different etymology. This may be worth mentioning at the outset otherwise you'll likely have one or two students who'll want to argue about the op-ed's true meaning. While this is an enjoyable endeavor—and good for students who know—the potential for descension into tangent-land is high.

There are many versions of op-ed assignments. They can be written from a historical perspective in which students pretend they are erstwhile actors or even themselves traveling back in time to assert opinions of their own. Maybe they're an American founder like James Madison, Alexander Hamilton, or John Jay debating the merits of the newly minted Constitution, or maybe they're oneself doing the same.

Op-eds can also be contemporary. Students pick a present-day issue and support their assertions with evidence learned during the most recent unit of study. In U.S. history, for example, assign an essay about a current inequality using the civil rights movement as evidence. In economics have students write about the best monetary and fiscal policy tools to increase growth and lower unemployment in today's economy. In geography task students with applying their knowledge of ethnocentrism and cultural pluralism to a contemporaneous global conflict.

Here's the kicker: when students are finished require they submit their work to a real-life publication like a local newspaper or national magazine. Who knows, you'll tell them, if your op-ed is published it might even help you get into college; at the very least it's a cool resume booster and a feather in your cap. Consider not grading the op-ed until students show you proof of submission (which can be as simple as a carbon copy on an email). Knowing that humans other than their teacher will potentially read their writing is an incredible motivator and a nice trick to entice students into taking the assignment more seriously.

Now that you've made the writing real what remains are the specifics such as word count, thesis, due date, etc. In addition to distributing a rubric and descriptor, like the ones included at the end of this chapter, you'll also want to familiarize students with the genre. Photocopy cuttings of curated op-eds or simply instruct students to visit websites of various media outlets. Have them spend some time reading then debrief their observations about form and writing style. Emphasize finding your voice, and compare style in writing to style of dress.

Not only is the op-ed a valuable assignment; it's also a vehicle for students to communicate their beliefs over the course of their entire lives—a method of participating in our democracy and contributing to the shared marketplace of ideas. Op-eds can spread through society like a virus, infecting those with even the most indirect contact; they can topple dictators and inspire the masses. If op-eds are powerful enough to change the world, surely they're appropriate for the social studies classroom as well.

III. BOOK REVIEW

Are you ever embarrassed to assign book reports because of their stigma? Do they feel juvenile, even reductive? Well, you are not alone. The traditional book report is often the subject of mockery—some warranted, some not—in part because it exists solely in the realm of education. Have you ever read a published book report? Of course not, because they do not exist. But what you and millions of Americans certainly have read is a book review.

The book review is an established and pervasive form of writing. There are entire magazines devoted to book reviews exclusively. They are regularly published in the world's best newspapers. Book reviews have the capacity to influence not just an author's esteem and material well-being but also the reach of an idea, so why not introduce them to students?

The constituent elements of a book review are the summary, evaluation, and publishing details. The summary is really more like background or context—the appetizer to the entree. It should provide enough information to advise the reader of the nature of the work without giving too much away. This might include main characters and theme and, especially for nonfiction, a sketch of the book's thesis and key evidence, so the reader has an idea of the route they will travel without detailing every step along the way.

Next is the evaluation. The reviewer should share their opinion of the book including what worked and what didn't, if the controlling argument stood up to scrutiny, and whether the style of writing held any appeal. Was the story told refreshingly? Was it a slog or an enjoyable read? Did the author advance a novel idea or illuminate some worthy moment in history? What effect, if any, will this book have on our understanding of the world?

Book reviews usually conclude with information like the publisher, page count, and price listed below the title and author's name. (Reviews also begin with an enticing title of their own.) Ultimately the purpose of a book review is to provide a service to potential readers, to both appraise and apprise.

There is a catch however. One must actually *read* a book in order to review it. Which means teachers should also consider an associated independent reading project. Books related to social studies will skew toward nonfiction, though historical fiction is an obvious exception. Letting students choose their books, like selecting a subject to research, is a nice way of increasing interest and buy-in. Any opportunity to imbue students with a love of reading is an opportunity worth seizing because as we know, good readers make good writers.

To properly read a book during the school year along with all the other demands of life and curriculum requires several months' time. Reading occasionally in class, like on Mondays for several consecutive weeks, will help hook students into their books. After that decide how much time in and out of class to allot for reading. Also consider some midway check-in assignment asking students to provide an update on how many pages they've read, what new words and content they've learned, and some personal connection to the text.

When the time comes, set a date by which the book should be read and the review completed. If you'd like, require that students submit their reviews for publication as with their op-eds. Maybe mention that people even get paid for reviews accepted at newspapers and magazines. More broadly remember to connect this assignment to writing in the real world. There's a genuine demand in society for learned book reviews from thoughtful people. Students should try one on, and see if it fits.

IV. HISTORICAL FICTION ESSAY

If historical fiction is suitable for students to read maybe it's also a genre in which they would like to write. Though most social studies writing is nonfiction, the historical fiction essay is a notable exception. It also requires research, an essential social studies skill.

At the end of a particular unit, or even a semester or year, students will investigate primary sources for accounts of interesting people, places, and events, using them as inspiration for a story of their own. Maybe they imagine two brothers fighting on opposite sides of the Mexican-American War, a teenager and her grandmother caught in the middle of the Haitian Revolution, an upstart inventor laboring in the Age of Enlightenment. Students won't cite sources in-text like a research paper, but they'll include a list of references they've used at the end, much like novelists do with books of their own.

For that matter why stop with an essay? Why not turn their short story into something longer? If working with an English teaching partner, this is a wonderful opportunity for project-based learning and collaboration across disciplines. The English teacher will naturally emphasize narrative arc and literary style while you focus on research and historical fidelity.

Or not. Or keep the assignment for yourself and emphasize the story in hi*story* (and perhaps it's patriarchal etymology while you're at it). Historical fiction is a delicious genre because one gets the best of both worlds: the forward propulsion of a narrative embedded in a particular period of time. It's no coincidence—history is indeed a story. And stories are how humans learn best. This is a lesson all teachers should keep front-of-mind, and the historical fiction essay is a great way to emphasize it with students while also improving their ability to write.

V. MAGAZINE PROJECT

Like the historical fiction essay, a magazine also has the potential to bleed into English curriculum, though it doesn't have to. Journalism occupies a middle ground between English and social studies, and with just a bit of instruction, students can create excellent magazines of their own.

Once again this project can be a summative assessment for any unit of study. The Supreme Court, Latin American foreign policy, apartheid, all have been the subjects of actual magazines many times over. Students might create cover pages, advertisements, letters to the editor, editor's notes, subscription mail inserts, crosswords, sudoku, horoscopes, pop-ups—anything one finds in a magazine. These items are endless fun. But the main writing will consist of feature essays.

Features should address a salient issue or theme, though they can also exist as profiles of individual people. Here again research is key. Good reporting must be flawless on the facts. In addition to consulting primary and secondary sources, students will also need to conduct interviews—primary sources themselves—in order to learn information on background and harvest usable quotes. This is likely the only discrete skill you'll have to introduce, assuming students are already familiar with analytical writing and source citation.

Style is also fairly loose. More informal than a research paper, a feature essay should feel natural, even intimate. It should strike a balance between conversational storytelling and clear-eyed scrutiny. (Not that the two are mutually exclusive.) There is more creative freedom found in a feature than a news article, for example, because magazine readers are willing to take time to get to know a subject whereas articles must be compact and to the point. This is about genre and what one expects when reading a certain type of writing.

For this reason the best way for students to familiarize themselves with the contours of a feature is to read as many feature essays as they can. Provide this opportunity in class or at home and have students discuss what they observe. In real life, feature requirements will vary from publication to publication, so setting wider guidelines is not a bad idea. Maybe simply a word count, one interview, and cited sources. Consider mentioning the importance of a hook to draw the reader in, an explicit controlling idea if not an overt thesis, and an organizational structure that allows for clarity, continuity, and a smooth flow.

The magazine project can be done alone, in groups, or as an entire class. Groups of three to five students are often most effective, but the whole-class version is an enjoyable undertaking too. Magazines online or in print work equally well. You may also want to highlight the connection between features and op-eds since both allow first-person usage in addition to significant flexibility in substance and style, even if the latter more conspicuously advances an argument.

If students are in need of motivation, talk about the fourth branch of government. About the importance of a free media to hold the powerful accountable, to spotlight overlooked issues and speak for the voiceless. In any healthy democracy the public must be informed, and there's no substitute for an active constellation of newspapers, broadcasters, and magazines (no, social media does not suffice). This is your students' chance to apply what they've learned in a way that's not just real, but also the very foundation of republican society itself. Plus they'll improve their writing in the process. Now what could be more compelling than that?

VI. WHITE PAPER

A white paper is a report. Specifically, an authoritative report from the government. Now also deployed by businesses and nonprofits, white papers take their name from the original administrative color on which they were printed (there are less well-known green, blue, and yellow papers as well). In essence a white paper is nothing more than a persuasive essay. It's a position paper, a concise statement of opinion, position, or policy intended to convince and persuade, educate and inform.

For these reasons white papers are ideally situated for government and economics classes, though one can imagine them in use in history, geography, law, and psychology courses as well. Show students examples of the genre to illustrate that this writing exists in the world, outside the classroom. Winston Churchill's 1922 report on Arab and Jewish conflict in Palestine is an early classic. Or try a more modern Securities and Exchange Commission analysis of municipal bonds.

What white papers lack in linguistic effervescence they make up for in precision and control. White papers are about advancing data in support of a position or elucidating a previously misunderstood issue; they seek solutions to problems and an educated readership. There is unquestionably a place for this type of writing in the classroom. Bordering on the technical it requires clear thinking and an economy of words. Say no more than is absolutely imperative, but don't leave anything out.

Students can write white papers as summative end-of-unit assessments, either stand alone or as part of a more comprehensive project. In a government executive branch unit, for example, groups of students might assume the role of cabinet members and write position papers to be considered by the teacher-president. The Department of Agriculture might pitch a particular policy on rural development, which must then be defended in front of the class.

In a macroeconomics unit, students can write papers suggesting a particular monetary policy in response to current economic conditions or put forward a position on the tension between unemployment and inflation. For a world history class, students could assume the role of Prince Metternich at the Congress of Vienna and interpret his views on the balance of power in Europe, while geography students impersonate Peace Corps leadership to address paths toward greater cultural understanding in Southeast Asia.

Whatever the subject, students should appreciate the utility of being able to write a concise report. The more authoritative, the better. Audiences are more likely to believe sources they trust and one way of becoming trustworthy is by writing well. To educate and persuade is to make a difference. In government or outside it, as part of a corporation or nonprofit, people write white papers to effect change. To make others see the world in a particular way, a way that aligns with the author's views. This is certainly something social studies students should learn how to do. Even if you're simply dressing the persuasive essay in formal new clothes, it's a good look.

VII. LEGAL BRIEF

Legal briefs are not just for law school. It isn't too much of a stretch to characterize briefs as another form of analytical essay since they seek to resolve an issue through argument and evidence. Beginning with a summary of the facts, briefs identify a central legal question and then answer that question through logic. Exactly the sort of writing that is endemic to social studies.

If you're teaching an elective like street law, the legal brief is a no-brainer. A sophomore who has requested representation is detained and searched by admin without his parents; a teenage girl encourages her friend to punch another girl, who suffers a brain injury as a result; a fast-food company is sued for serving extra-spicy food. Students can write—and argue—about similar cases ad infinitum.

But in history, government, geography, and economics, the brief is equally effective and still highly relevant. With only the slightest massaging, students can write briefs in support of controversial historical events or in opposition to current domestic policy. For example, Was Napoleon a friend or foe of the French revolution? Why not put him on trial, with a written summary of the significant facts and rationale as support?

After the Civil War the United States promised coastal land in South Carolina, Georgia, and Florida to African Americans. Should General William Tecumsah Sherman's Field Order Number 15 have been overturned by President Andrew Jackson, reneging on the government's promise of reparations via "40 acres and a mule"? Young Americans sue for action on climate change, alleging violations of their constitutional rights. Should they prevail? Minnesota considers passage of a state law increasing the minimum wage. Will raising the pay floor harm small businesses and ultimately damage the economy?

Indeed it's difficult to imagine a social studies course in which legal briefs have no application. All classes should help students learn how to write effectively, and the brief is a spin on the analytical essay that is not only authentic but also a nice occasion for students to support their own opinions with arguments and evidence. Comprising a fact summary, a legal question, and an answer, briefs can assume a variety of forms to meet your needs. They can be written independently or in groups, in class or at home. They can be as lengthy or as (brief!) as you desire. They're also our final example of real-world persuasive essay writing.

VIII. FAMILY HISTORY RESEARCH PROJECT

Why not a family history? Why not write about one's ancestry and how they came to live in this—or any other—country? In truth this project is also analytical since one's family history must still be proven, but the personal nature of such writing lends it an immediacy and relevance that may be lacking in even the most captivating of theoretical discourses.

Building on students' knowledge of academic research methods, family histories are among the most direct means of students seeing themselves in the curriculum. Though most clearly aligned with American history, such research could also occur in world history, geography, maybe even government.

In this case students will be supplied with their topic and research question. How did my family and I come to live in (this town, this state, this country)? Clearly, personal exceptions should be made for students without families, exchange students, or anyone else uncomfortable for any reason with the assignment. Personal exploration is by definition sensitive, and teachers should be sensitive to the personal struggles of students. Or more succinctly, since the personal is sensitive, be sensitive to the personal (long live the chiasmus).[1]

Armed with a guiding question, students should research until they generate a thesis and sufficient evidence to prove it. One advantage of personal research is the reduced imperative to rely on the internet. In-person interviews, oral histories, archival photos, documents, artifacts, and memorabilia are all excellent sources of information. Think about a Polish family emigration legend, a faded black-and-white photograph of Armenian great grandparents, a branding iron from the Rocking Chair Ranch in eastern Arizona. All tell a story about where one came to live and how one came to be.

Family histories also speak to the salience of local history. The story of a place can add much needed context to the story of a family and an individual. Is one descended from the indigenous Coast Miwok? How about from the Spanish of Alta California, from Irish or Chinese immigrants during the Gold Rush, or African Americans during the shipbuilding boom of World War II? All these stories are true of Northern California, for example, giving texture to a place and therefore also to the people who inhabit it.

By connecting students' own lives to the town, state, and country in which they live, the family research project helps students see themselves in our curriculum, in the broader narrative of America. Such investigation also brings up weighty questions like the true nature of America's identity and what it means to be an American. It connects people with their community, both large and small.

Family research also sharpens students' academic skills in a way that is personally relevant in the extreme. Though such thoughts are far from the teenage mind, students may one day find themselves engaged in similar work purely for their own edifying pleasure. Everyday across the country, and for that matter the globe, adults plumb the depths of their ancestral identity to better understand who they are and from whence they came. At least once over the course of their academic career, students should engage in this worthy pursuit, while at the same time also improving their ability to write.

IX. MEMOIR

Memoir, from the French cognate for memory, is an immensely popular genre residing along the spectrum closer to but not necessarily wholly apart from fiction. Like the family history research project, the memoir allows students to uncover truths about themselves, with an emphasis on storytelling and the narrative arc. Memoirs benefit from rising and falling action, a climax, and a denouement—a trajectory to keep the reader engaged.

Memoirs can recount one's entire existence, an era, or a discrete event. The cinematic sweep of a lifetime spent lobbying for women's suffrage, the tumult of growing up as a child during the Cultural Revolution, or the adventures of a left-handed pitcher in the first and only season of professional baseball in Israel. There are virtually no rules and no limits. The memoir is a liberation.

Though you might think memoir writing is a stretch for social studies courses, consider these ideas. In government, students write stories of their political activism; in economics, chronicles of their personal financial literacy; in geography, accounts of interactions with foreign cultures or the way in which the local terrain has influenced who they have become. Telling stories that dovetail course content with students' lived experiences is always an effective approach.

Research is also a component of memoir writing, affording students yet another opportunity to practice this valuable skill. And if you share students with an English teaching partner, the memoir, like the historical fiction essay, is a wonderful way to collaborate across curricula.

Memoirs help us understand who we are. They replenish our soul. There comes a time in every person's life when they consider committing at least a portion of their existence to the page. These stories can also reveal much about the era in which one lived. If students learn to value memoir writing for the insight it brings into their own lives as well as the world around them, this assignment will have been well worth the effort.

X. SPEECH

In some ways a speech is simply a spoken essay. There have been infinite unwritten speeches, of course, the extemporaneous lecture, the ad-libbed disquisition, the unscripted diatribe on any number of subjects. But many speeches, especially the planned ones, have first been put in writing.

If students want to learn how to deliver a good speech, they must also learn how to write one. The process is much the same as a standard essay—brainstorm, outline, write a first draft, revise, and polish—with the added step of returning the work to outline form. Speeches are clearly intended to be more conversational than essays, which is important to keep in mind for both the drafting and revising stages. Write the speech like you'd talk. Don't spend unnecessary time rescripting the perfect prose because no one will see your words anyway—they're only going to hear them.

Actually writing out a speech is not necessary in all instances, but for assignments and especially summative assessments, it should be a requirement. This is also a good way to monitor student progress and offer formative feedback. What's more, students will feel less pressure both writing conversationally and knowing their drafts will eventually be reduced back down to bulleted form.

Presentations in which students recite directly from a densely typed page can feel like witnessing a car crash in slow motion. You know you shouldn't stare, but it's hard to look away. Fearing they will forget what to say, students often ensnare themselves in a classic trap of their own making: writing too much down. They must never read their speech, whether printed out, pasted onto notecards, or glowing from a smartphone screen.

Instead, bulleted outlines offer a more effective form of written aid. Outlines can be structured or informal but with an economy of words. The outline is merely a cue, a reminder, a gentle nudge—and emphatically not a transcript to be dictated.

Students should endeavor to be human and conversational when speaking in front of an audience. They should use volume, inflection, pacing, and tone, gestures, posture, and eye contact, to add to the meaning of their words. They should know that even though they'll first need to write their speech, at the end of the day they'll be saying it.

XI. VISUAL ESSAY

True, the lion's share of a visual essay is not writing per se. But it's a recognized method of storytelling and an engaging way for students to summatively apply what they have learned. Visual essays are also not completely devoid of writing. Words accompany graphics and images—they're just not the primary focus.

In their most straightforward incarnation, visual essays are composed of a scroll of images and captions. The images can be primary- or secondary-source photographs, drawings, maps, annotations, or cartoons. If the visual essay is digital, it might also include gifs (yes, gifs) as well as videos or interactive features. Maybe the format is not a scroll but some other setup entirely. You can decide how many visuals students should include and how much writing is required to support them.

Teachers know that students sometimes need alternate avenues to communicate their ideas. The benefit of a visual essay is that it allows students to convey and support an argument in a less traditionally academic fashion. After all who isn't familiar with the axiom that a picture is worth a thousand words? Students who gain confidence expressing themselves visually may also eventually become more comfortable writing. These students can transition from captions to paragraphs to full-length essays.

Plus even visual artists must be able to write. An artist's statement, for example, is a written explanation of their work. It conveys through language the ideas of an exhibit, a specific piece, or one's entire career.

Though the visual essay is not writing as literally understood, it still requires students to make and defend an argument. And it's important for them to know that pictures, including motion pictures and other art forms, are capable of the same. Hopefully, students will enjoy this respite from conventional writing while continuing to think deeply and critically, and at the same time gain confidence in other forms of communication.

XII. COMICS

Finally, the comic. The rationale for writing comics is the same as for the visual essay. (You could take this a step further and explain to students the difference between semiotics and linguistics—the study of signs and symbols versus the study of language—to justify the comic's pedagogical value, but that's less than necessary.)

At its most elemental a comic is sequential art. Students should know comics are not infographics. They're not posters or cartoons. Comic strips are almost always divided into multiple panels or frames which can be of similar or different sizes. Many but not all panels will include both images and words, drawings and dialogue.

For one reason or another, comics are a medium of storytelling to which young people are naturally drawn. Take advantage of this truth and assign comics as either summative or formative assessments, at the end of a unit or as part of a one-off lesson. Class is often at its most pleasant when students are drawing, chatting peacefully with their peers, all the while engaged in your content. (Indeed we have much to admire of our colleagues in the fine arts.)

Like other real-world writing, comics fit a variety of curricular needs. Microeconomics, Japanese-American internment, the Star Spangled Banner, ethnocentrism, absolute and relative location, the Industrial Revolution—it is difficult to imagine a subject matter with which comics are incompatible.

And if you enjoy assigning comics to students, you might also consider their muscular cousin, the graphic novel. Or why not cross-pollinate? Why not experiment with a graphic memoir, an op-ed comic, or a magazine of book reviews? As with teaching social studies writing in general, the framework is paramount. Discover other writing that exists outside the classroom, like novels, anthologies, and blogs, and mimic them, adapt them to your curriculum. Students will be more highly motivated to write in a manner they believe is real.

While there is surely inherent value in traditional academic analysis, real-world writing offers the promise of seduction. The potential for students to see their work as authentic, even transcendental. Because in the end we don't just want students to learn to write, we want them to love it.

KEY IDEAS

- Nonfiction writing is integral to social studies.
- Adapting real-world genres to the classroom is an effective practice because students will be more highly motivated and thus more likely to improve their writing skills in a meaningful way.
- Examples include op-eds, book reviews, historical fiction essays, magazine features, white papers, legal briefs, family histories, memoirs, speeches, visual essays, and comics.
- Experiment with additional forms of authentic writing to boost student engagement and ability.

NOTE

1. For those partial to classroom tangents, there is no better fodder than fine words and the histories behind them. "Chiasmus," for example, stems from the Greek letter "chi," which is shaped like an "x," connoting a crosswise or inverted syntactical relationship. My how wonderful are words—lexophiles unite!

Op-Ed

"The pen is mightier than the sword."—Edward Bulwer-Lytton, 1839

Your task

You will write an op-ed in which you address a current issue related to our unit of study. It should be 750–1,000 words in length.

You need to include:

- A clear argument; evidence from, but not limited to, what we have learned this unit; analysis of your evidence; all necessary citations

The writing process:

- (1) Brainstorm (2) Research (3) Outline (4) Write (5) Revise

Once finished you will submit your op-ed to be published (like actually published!). You can submit anywhere you'd like such as our school's newspaper, our town's local paper, *The Washington Post*, *The Los Angeles Times*, AL.com, etc. But be sure to share evidence of your submission with me.

What does Op-Ed mean?

Op-ed comes from "opposite editorial" as in opposite the editorial page of a newspaper. It's often also thought of as "opinion editorial" which is correct in meaning if not etymology.

Now read several examples of op-ed essays from various media outlets to get a feel for the genre. What do you notice about them?

Book Review

This semester you have been reading a book of your choosing that is related to the content of this course. To show what you've learned, and as a way of processing what you've read, you will write a book review. This is quite different from the traditional book report.

The main elements of a book review are: (1) Summary (2) Evaluation (3) Publishing Details.

Summary: The summary is really more like background or context. It's the appetizer to the entree. It should provide enough information to advise the reader of the nature of the work without giving too much away. This might include main characters and themes. (Nonfiction books will also feature a sketch of the thesis and key evidence so the reader has an idea of the route they will travel without detailing every step along the way.)

Evaluation: The reviewer should share their opinion of the book. This could cover what worked and what didn't, if the thesis was well proven, and whether the style of writing was appealing. Also, consider these questions: Was the story told refreshingly? Was it a slog or an enjoyable read? Did the author advance a novel idea or illuminate some worthy moment in history? What effect if any will this book have on our understanding of the world?

Publishing details: Book reviews usually conclude with information like the publisher, page count, and price listed below the title and author's name. (Reviews also begin with an enticing title of their own.)

Ultimately the purpose of a book review is to provide a service to potential readers, to both evaluate and inform.

What is the title of your book? How are you enjoying it so far?

Historical Fiction Essay

History is mostly about what actually happened in the past. History is non-fiction. Yet historical fiction is still an immensely popular book genre. With historical fiction, you get the best of both worlds: the forward propulsion of a narrative embedded in a particular period of time.

It's no coincidence—hi*story* is indeed a story. And stories are how humans learn best. So let's invent some historical fiction of our own. Rather than a book you'll write an essay, or short story. And since it's historical you'll need to do some research.

Begin by investigating primary sources for accounts of interesting people, places, and events, and use them as inspiration for your own unique story. (Yes, real-life authors really do conduct research before starting to write.)

Unlike a formal research paper, you won't have to cite sources in the body of your story. But you'll still need to include a list of references you've used at the end (again, much like novelists do with books of their own).

Here are the specifics. Your story should be: fictional; historical; based on primary source research; related in some way to the content of the course; at least 2,000 words long.

Use the space below to brainstorm.
What eras of history are you most interested in?

What kind of story do you want to tell?

Do you have any ideas about characters or the plot?

Magazine Project

Your task is to create a magazine illustrating your understanding of the main issues and ideas from this unit. You will work in groups of four and you can choose groups yourself. Your grade will be based on your knowledge of the unit we have just studied in general and on your specific performance in particular. (See the rubric.)

Each person will write an article, create an ad, and make an "extra."

Article: You will write about one aspect of the unit. Make sure your issue is both relevant and significant. Your article should be 1,000–1,500 words long and include research and an interview. I will provide further information on both.

Advertisement: You will create an ad that is relevant to the unit. (It doesn't need to be related to your article.)

Extra: The purpose of your extra is to make your magazine seem real. Here are some ideas: the cover; editor's note (introduction); a "letters" section where real or imaginary people write in to your magazine; a foldout section; word search or crossword puzzle; horoscopes; business reply mail card; final thought (at the back of your magazine). Do you have another cool idea? Let me know.

Whole magazine: These are in addition to the specific requirements for each role. They are: an attractive cover with an interesting title; page numbers; table of contents; name or initials on each ad, extra, and article (so I know who did what); binding (such as lamination, stapling, rings, a booklet, etc.)

To review, each person will write an article; create an advertisement; make an "extra" for your section.

White Paper

A white paper is a report. To be specific, it's an authoritative report from the government. (If you're curious, the term "white paper" comes from the original administrative color on which it was printed. There are even less well-known green, blue, and yellow papers as well).

In essence, a white paper is a persuasive essay. It's a position paper, a concise statement of opinion or policy intended to convince and persuade an audience—like the president or the State Department.

White papers are about advancing data in support of a position or clarifying a previously misunderstood issue. They require clear thinking and an economy of words. Say no more than is absolutely imperative, but don't leave anything out.

Hopefully you can appreciate the usefulness of being able to write a concise report. The more authoritative, the better. People are more likely to believe sources they trust and one way of becoming trustworthy is by writing well.

So let's all write a white paper! In groups of one, you will pick a current issue that's related to our unit of study. And you'll use what you've learned from this unit to support your argument.

Requirements: No more than 1,000 words long; research; in-text source citations; a bibliography.

Use the space below to brainstorm possible subjects and positions.

_____
_____
_____
_____
_____
_____
_____
_____
_____
_____
_____
_____
_____
_____
_____
_____
_____
_____
_____

Legal Brief

Legal briefs are not only for law school. A brief is basically just another form of analytical essay in that it seeks to resolve an issue through argument and evidence.

Elements of a legal brief:

• Summarize the facts
• Identify the central question at issue
• Answer the question through persuasion and logic

As you can see this is very much like the writing we already do. In groups of three, you will write a brief about one contentious issue from this unit.

Process:

• (1) Identify an issue. (2) Phrase the issue as a question. (3) Conduct research to help you answer the question. (4) Write the brief.

Requirements:

• Research; in-text source citations; a bibliography; 1,000–1,500 words long

Note that in the real world, briefs can be as lengthy or as (brief!) as one wants.

Consider these various examples: Is a teenage girl who encourages her friend to punch another girl, who then suffers a brain injury as a result, criminally liable? Can a fast-food company be successfully sued for serving extra-spicy food? Was Napoleon a friend or foe of the French Revolution? Should General Sherman's Field Order Number 15 have been overturned by President Jackson, thereby reneging on the promise of reparations for African Americans after the Civil War? Will raising the minimum wage harm small businesses and damage the economy?

Family History Research Project

Who doesn't want to learn about who they are and where they're from? Most of us are our own most interesting subject. So let's dig into our family history while also improving our research skills in the process.

The key steps in writing a research paper are: select a topic; develop a research question; decide on a notetaking style; conduct research; learn or review paraphrasing versus direct quotes; learn or review source evaluation techniques; craft a thesis; make an outline; learn or review citation methods; write the first draft; edit and revise; produce a final copy.

Through your research and ultimately your paper, you will try to answer this question: *How did my family and I come to live in (this town, this state, this country)?*

Note: Please see me if for personal reasons you do not feel comfortable with this project. That's totally fine—we'll come up with an alternate assignment for you to do.

Pro tip: In-person interviews, oral histories, archival photos, documents, artifacts, and memorabilia are all excellent sources of information.

And who knows, someday when you're much much older—like really old, like in your thirties or even your forties or fifties, and let's not even mention your sixties or seventies, you just might find yourselves engaged in similar research purely for your own interest and pleasure.

List any initial ideas below about who you'll talk to or where you'll start looking.

_____

_____

_____

_____

_____

_____

_____

_____

_____

_____

_____

_____

_____

_____

_____

_____

Memoir

Did you know that "memoir" comes from the French word *mémoire*, which means memory? That's really all memoirs are—your written memories. Memoirs help us understand who we are. They allow us to uncover truths about ourselves, with an emphasis on storytelling and the narrative arc.

Memoirs benefit from these elements: rising action; falling action; a climax; a resolution; an overall plot or trajectory to keep the reader engaged; research.

These stories can also reveal much about the era in which we live. Memoir writing can bring insight into our own lives as well as the world around us. So for this unit you will tell a story of your life that dovetails with what we've learned.

Consider these examples: The experience of a suffragette fighting for women's right to vote. The childhood of a young girl growing up during the Chinese Cultural Revolution. The adventures of a pitcher in the first and only season of Israeli professional baseball. Your history of political activism. Your relationship with money. Your interactions with people from foreign cultures.

To be sure, there comes a time in every person's life when they consider committing at least a portion of their existence to the page. For you, that time is now.

Use the space below to begin brainstorming.

Speech

As our summative assessment, you will deliver a four-to-seven minute speech applying what you believe are the most important lessons from this unit to the present day.

The process for writing a speech is much like a traditional essay—brainstorm, outline, write a first draft, revise, and polish—except with one caveat: when you're done you'll return it to outline form. Remember that no one (other than your teacher and a peer editor) is going to see your speech, so don't stress about writing perfect sentences. What matters most is how it *sounds*.

Public speaking tips: Be conversational; speak *to* your audience, not *at* them; consider your voice's volume, pacing, inflection, and tone; ensure your body language adds to the meaning of your words; make appropriate eye contact (Goldilocks rule); do not read from your notes (especially not the typewritten speech itself); use natural gestures; think about your posture and movement; know that what you say is no more important than how you say it!

Use the space below to get started on step one, brainstorming.

Visual Essay

For this unit you will create an essay addressing a current issue related to what we have been studying. The rub is that your essay will be *visual*.

Option 1: The scroll. In their most straightforward version, visual essays are composed of a scroll of images and captions. The images can be primary- or secondary-source photographs, drawings, maps, annotations, or cartoons. If your essay is digital, it might also include gifs (yes, gifs) as well as videos.

Option 2: Avant-garde. You can also design a new format entirely. Maybe it's not a linear scroll, maybe it's interactive, maybe it's something mind-blowingly experimental.

Whichever you choose, your visual essay should have a main idea that you attempt to prove. You're still making and defending an argument. This is similar to the way songs and movies communicate ideas.

Note: Visual essays are not completely devoid of writing. Words will accompany graphics and images—they're just not the primary focus.

What is our current unit of study?

_____
_____
_____
_____
_____
_____
_____
_____
_____

Use the space below to brainstorm and generate ideas.

_____
_____
_____
_____
_____
_____
_____
_____
_____
_____
_____
_____
_____
_____

Comics

For this unit you will create a comic to illustrate—get it, illustrate?—what you've learned. If you think comics are just silly drawings, think again. Comics are an ancient form of communication, and they're immensely popular around the world. And if you're still not convinced, consider that "semiotics" is an entire discipline devoted to the study of signs and symbols (as opposed to "linguistics," which is the study of language).

At its most elemental, a comic is sequential art. Comics are not infographics. They're not posters or cartoons. Comic strips are almost always divided into multiple panels or frames which can be of similar or different sizes. Many but not all panels will include both images and words, drawings and dialogue.

What is our current unit of study?

_____

_____

_____

_____

_____

_____

_____

Use the space below to brainstorm and generate ideas. Think about how you'll answer the essential question of the unit. (Since you're making a comic, feel free to brainstorm visually.)

Chapter 7

Writing as Assessment

Grading papers today? Remember that you're a writing teacher, not a copy editor.

—Carol Jago

I. GRADING PRINCIPLES

Assigning writing is one thing, grading it is another entirely. There are so many issues, dilemmas, and considerations when it comes to grading student work that it's difficult to know where to begin. What makes sense is to start with a general philosophy, followed by a set of principles, to guide teachers through the myriad decisions that inevitably surface along the way.

At their most fundamental, grading systems should be *fair and accurate*. Teachers want to give students the grade they deserve, assuming students have had a reasonable opportunity to earn the C+ or A−. It is possible to give both an accurate grade that is unfair, and a fair grade that is inaccurate. So we must strive for both.

To achieve these dual goals, teachers should *set clear expectations and provide opportunities for improvement*. Setting clear expectations is fairly straightforward. Distribute an assignment descriptor and a rubric and explain both, answering questions as you proceed. In addition, provide student models to make your abstract guidelines more concrete. Students will be able to see examples of work you deem advanced, proficient, basic, etcetera.

It's also a nice idea to allow students multiple chances to show what they've learned. Even on summative assessments like end-of-unit essays. If someone wants to improve, even if their true motivation is a better grade and not superior skills or greater knowledge, why not let them try? (Hint: most students won't.) In this way grading systems not only measure but actually *increase* student learning.

This is as true of assessing writing as it is of unit tests, projects, and homework. Aim to be fair and accurate, set clear expectations, and let students turn in assignments more than once—even if only a few will actually take advantage of your beneficence.

II. THE "REAL-REAL"

Assessments can be authentic, artificial, or somewhere in between. This spectrum has been referred to as "real-real" "fake-real," and "real-fake," and even if you don't love the terminology, the ideas behind it are instructive. Think back to the difference between academic and real-world writing (and recall that both are not necessarily mutually exclusive). Authentic assignments are those that could or actually do exist outside the classroom.

Assigning an op-ed that students must submit for publication is "real-real" in that any other citizen not in school has the ability to do the same. Tackling a littering problem on campus via the school newspaper or sending white papers to the town council to address criminal justice reform are inherently authentic too.

But such projects can be time consuming and overly ambitious, and sometimes it's better to mimic a real-world action than to actually undertake one. These "fake-real" assignments ask students to pretend they are writing outside the classroom when really they're just turning something in. There is absolutely nothing wrong with this. Making writing seem real, giving it the feel of authenticity, also greatly increases student motivation. You assign the op-ed, for example, but don't make students submit it; you have students create magazines but not for public consumption; you ask students to write reports as if they'll be sent to the town council.

And finally the "real-fake," a term which happens to be unnecessarily pejorative. Another word for fake or inauthentic would be academic, and as the first half of this book argues there is immense value in academic writing. Academic writing is difficult, necessary, and highly transferable, and therefore also relevant to students' lives. The connection is more attenuated, however, so it's likely students will be less motivated and less excited. And who's to say academic is inauthentic in the first place? There are plenty of meaningful and remunerative real-world professions in academia including professors, researchers, and administrators.

So don't let the phrase "real-fake" dissuade you. The point is to understand its place in the social studies curriculum. Reflect on the needs of your students and chose among real-world, real-world-inspired, and academic writing to meet the goals you wish to achieve.

III. FORMATIVE VERSUS SUMMATIVE

Yet another consideration is whether student writing will be formative or summative. That is to say whether it will occur leading up to the final evaluation (formative) or whether it will be the final evaluation itself (summative).

Most of the academic and real-world writing discussed in chapters 4, 5, and 6 falls into the summative category. These assignments generally come at the end of a four-to-six week unit of study. They're intended to both improve students' writing skills and provide an outlet to demonstrate what particular content has been learned. As mentioned in chapter 1 this approach is known as *teaching skills through content*. DBQs, research papers, book reviews, historical fiction essays, white papers, and memoirs are all examples of summative assessments.

Formative assessments are the practice—the check-ins to note student progress and provide directional feedback. Weekly analytical paragraph writing, notetaking, annotating, research, source analysis, outlines, drafts of essays, all are formative in nature.

At this point it's worth mentioning the elephant in the room. The elephant conceivably weighing down each and every page. How on earth is one expected to grade so much writing? I can't even get through my stacks of essays to begin with, you may be thinking, There's no way I can handle anything more! The answer, in part, is this: You do not have to grade everything you assign. Much of the formative writing students will do is just that—formative, as in relating to one's development. If students won't write unless affixed to their words is a numerical score that will eventually be entered into a gradebook, the issue becomes one of motivation and strategy.

There are many ways to get students to do what you want using both carrots and sticks. You can always threaten—"Don't force me to grade this," you'll say, "You guys don't want that and neither do I." But ideally you'll make students actually *want* to write. Tell them there's no pressure since there's no grade, that this is just practice anyway. Practice to prepare for the upcoming summative assessment, the research paper or in-class DBQ, but also practice for life—for the development of their critical thinking and analytical writing skills so they'll be more enlightened human beings as well as more coveted employees.

Feedback can also be informal in nature. Walk the room and while peeking over students' shoulders give them verbal feedback on the spot. "That needs a better topic sentence," or "Remember the period goes after the in-text parenthetical citation." Also, contemplate why you're providing feedback in the first place. Is it to justify the grade you've just marked on a paper, so students won't badger you with questions, or is it to help students improve so they'll do better next time? The former is certainly understandable and in some ways a practical necessity, but the latter is our sincere goal.

Therefore try providing as much efficient formative feedback as possible and as little summative feedback as required. Speak with students, either casually or in short, designated meetings, or write notes directly on their work, but worry less about assigning a grade. (Students are often distracted by the grade anyway and overlook the more important critiques and praise.) Keep in mind the natural tendency toward the opposite—more summative feedback, less formative—and continue to fight against this urge. Always remain cognizant of the type of feedback you're giving, and why.

IV. GRADING MECHANICS

Having thought through a general philosophy and approach, let's examine the actual specifics of grading social studies writing. Hopefully, students receive an assignment descriptor and rubric at the outset and informal feedback along the way. They've just submitted their essays and the stack is leaning conspicuously just to the right of your desk or clogging up your learning management system. Now is time to render judgement. True, you could merely write one of five letter grades in circled red ink at the top of the page, but you'd probably feel guilty and students and their parents might complain.

Instead do three things: annotate the paper, fill out the rubric, and conclude with a compliment sandwich. Don't annotate thoroughly, as if you were a college freshman wading headlong into your first inscrutable text, just make a few marks for your own clarity and so students will have proof you read each page. Better yet include an annotation guide at the back of your syllabus to start the year so students can decode your symbols. Underline means you're simply making note of something, like the thesis; checkmarks mean good; stars and exclamation points, great or very important; circles and xs, errors or mistakes.

But please avoid the impulse to copy edit. This, perhaps more than anything else, bogs down the grading process. If you must, simply circle the erratum and move on. Correcting students' mistakes does not help them learn anyway since resubmitted drafts will reflect your changes alone and not those of your students. Plus these are summative assessments not works in progress. Copy edit at your peril. Grade efficiently and clearly, and you're more likely to assign more writing, which will be of greater benefit to students in the long run.

After a few marks on the paper itself move to the rubric. Rubrics should have between three and five columns separating degrees of superior and less superior work. For example, advanced, proficient, basic, and less than satisfactory, which align with grades A, B, C, and D–F respectively. Each column should include various vertically bulleted criteria, linked to all other columns with varying adjectives.

Let's say the first bullet on your analytical essay rubric is the thesis. The advanced column will read "clear, specific, argumentative thesis"; the proficient column "mostly clear, specific, argumentative thesis"; the basic column "somewhat clear, specific, argumentative thesis"; and the less than satisfactory column "unclear, unspecific, unargumentative thesis." Feel free to vary the column names and adjectives and general criteria but ensure each bullet links in this way with the corresponding bullets in the other columns. Students will be able to comprehend very plainly and clearly each component of your evaluation.

Not only does a clear rubric help students understand the justification for their grade, but it also means they will be less likely to question your judgement. And if you're inclined to allow multiple attempts at summative assessments, a detailed rubric shows students exactly how they must improve—without actually doing the work for them (no copy editing!).

So after annotating, simply check, underline, or circle the bullets that apply in each column. At this point, if not earlier, you should know what grade the paper deserves. Write that grade somewhere on the rubric, and circle it to show students you mean business. By now you have done more than enough. Your efforts are nothing short of heroic.

But why not take an extra twenty seconds to write an open- or closed-face compliment sandwich proving to students how much you care? They've just written 1,127 words, more than they ever thought possible, so it's reasonable you write them a few in return. "Great hook! Make sure your thesis includes a counterargument." Or, "You include much great detail here. Very thorough. Your paper would benefit from more consistent analysis." If students do nothing else, if they disregard your rubric and overlook your annotations, they will review the grade and read your comments.

When students want to know why they received a particular grade, ask them to look over the rubric and repeat back the details of your assessment. You need not be snarky or condescending, even if a fire is burning in your belly. Instead, speak with respect and empathy just like students are—hopefully—speaking to you. Again, allow make-ups or not. If so you might require students write a one-paragraph response addressing how they performed and why they want to redo the assignment. This will engender reflection as well as create the tiniest of hurdles for students to jump.

Ideally, teachers should strive for grading systems that are not only fair and accurate but also efficient and clear. Students should know what grade they've received and why, and teachers should not burn out in the process. A graded essay which is annotated and stapled behind a tight, marked up rubric with written words of critique and praise will go a long way toward these ends.

V. GRADES VERSUS CHARACTER

Do you ever get nervous passing back papers? Maybe they're a month overdue, maybe you're second-guessing your initial judgement, maybe you're apprehensive about pushback from students. All completely understandable and not uncommon. Try tackling batches of five essays at a time rather than summoning the courage to face the entire pile at once; trust in your ability to assess; and greet questioning students firmly with solicitude.

The paper pass back can also be a rattling experience for students. Stealing glances at their classmates' essays and constantly comparing themselves against their peers. For students who earn stellar marks, receiving graded work is undoubtedly validating and joyous. But for those who are consistently presented with subpar, unsatisfactory, or middling scores, the entire affair must be worse than disheartening. Not only must they come to grips with not doing well, resigned to the reality of their teachers' similar view, but they must also answer to their peers. "What did you get? What did you get?" One can only imagine the trauma.

Inducing students to anguish and despair is not why we become teachers. Nonetheless, school is a meritocracy, and though we seek to level the playing field and ensure fair equality of opportunity, at the end of the day we're still compelled to evaluate student learning. Note, however, the emphasis on student *learning*—not the students themselves. We do not measure students, only their performance.

This is an important if subtle point to bear in mind. For better and worse, students often associate achievement with self-worth. And while we do educate the "whole child," the totality of a young person's value is not wrapped up in their sophomore world history grade. Too often teachers pass back papers and focus on short-term results to the detriment of the long-term psychology of their students.

Instead, we should overtly discuss what grades mean, and what they don't. Grades are not shorthand for moral value. Students who receive higher grades than other students are not better people, they've just performed better on a particular assignment or over the course of a certain class. Ranking the relative holistic merit of individual students might be an interesting exercise—something akin to the college application process—yet that's not what we're doing either.

Several times a semester, if not more frequently, teachers should speak with students about the significance of grades. That grades should not be confused with self-worth. There are many aspects to a good life well lived, and social studies achievement is but a sliver. This does not mean one should work any less hard, remain any less engaged, or strive to learn any less than their fullest potential. The reasons for doing so abound, including understanding oneself and one's place in the world, and becoming a more agile thinker and more capable writer. These pursuits will last a lifetime.

Some students are funny, some play the piano, others excel in math or basketball. Some speak three languages and others cook with their aging grandmother. All of our students are unique, and all of them matter. Don't let the grades you assign to them interfere with this truth. Don't let students believe they are valuable or not, worthy or not, according to their ability to write an analytical paragraph or research a primary source. Don't let students think you like some of them more than others because of the grades they receive. In the end a grade is an assessment of students' knowledge and skills, not a judgement on their character.

VI. GROWTH, GRIT, MENTAL TOUGHNESS

Lastly, in addition to knowing what a grade means and what it doesn't, students should learn how to persevere and improve. A grade is a data point, a moment in time. It does not confer an essence. One is not necessarily "good at writing" because one gets good grades on essays and vice versa.

Students should be taught that learning is not a fixed character trait. With determination and persistence—and good teaching—they can unquestionably improve. Around the time students receive formative feedback or summative grades is a nice occasion to reiterate this point.

And here we come full circle to an emphasis on the process. *Process over product.* The quickest path toward an outstanding product is a dogged emphasis on the process. A student is upset with her DBQ grade? Good. It's a heartening sign she wants to get better. Together you can examine her strengths and weaknesses on the assessment, and she can practice, then try again. How many young people have turned away from a subject or career because they believed they "weren't good at" science or math or history or writing? It's true that human beings have a natural aptitude toward some things more than others. But who cares?

Adolescence is not merely about finding something you're good at and sticking with it. (Who even knows what this is, anyway, at fourteen years of age?) Rather, students should strive to find subjects they enjoy, those that will prove meaningful to their lives and the communities in which they live.

Every one of us can improve ourselves and our skills. We all have the ability to grow. When students receive grades from their teachers, they should from time to time hear this lesson as well. Practice, get feedback, perform, grow. The caliber of one's mindset may be more important than the quality of one's mind. We should focus on the things we can control and leave the rest to the gods and fate. A grade is an opportunity. A chance to get better. A grade is an invitation.

KEY IDEAS

- Grading systems should be fair and accurate; teachers should set clear expectations and provide opportunities for improvement.
- Assessments can range from real-world to real-world-inspired to academic.
- Feedback on formative assessments is most conducive to increased student learning.
- When grading summative assessments, annotate the paper, fill out the rubric, and include written comments of critique and praise.
- It is important to separate students' academic achievement from their self-worth.
- Grades should be framed as an opportunity to practice positive mental habits such as grit, perseverance, and a growth mindset.

Teacher Feedback Guide

There are three main ways I will give you feedback this year: (1) On a rubric. (2) Verbally. (3) By marking up your work. In much the same way that you've learned how to annotate a reading, I will often do the same with your writing. Marking up your work allows me to efficiently make notes as I go, which both helps me grade and gives you some insight into why you received the score that you did. So take a look at the symbols and their meanings below, and expect to see at least some of them on your work this year.

Symbol	Meaning
✓	Good, nice, well done, generally positive. (You'll see a lot of check marks.)
O	Something is missing or needs to be fixed. I may circle a word, several words, or the space between words.
!	I love it, very cool, spot on. Exclamation points mean your work excites me.
X	Wrong. If I put an "X" through a word, or a sentence, or a paragraph, it means what you have written is incorrect.
☆	Yes, exactly, very good. Stars are extra special. They denote excellence.
_____	I may underline key words, phrases, and sentences (like your thesis). This helps me remember important parts of what you've written.

Final thought: I will give feedback which is both criticism and praise. The truth is that there is much to admire in ALL of our work. And it's also true that every one of us can continue to improve. Even if you get an A on an assignment, I will try to show you how you can get better.

Notetaking Rubric

Advanced	Proficient	Basic	Needs Improvement
Text's main idea is clearly evident	Text's main idea is mostly evident	Text's main idea is somewhat evident	Text's main idea is not evident
Appropriate supporting detail is provided	Appropriate supporting detail is mostly provided	Appropriate supporting detail is somewhat provided	Appropriate supporting detail is not provided
Superfluous detail is omitted	Superfluous detail is mostly omitted	Superfluous detail is somewhat omitted	Superfluous detail is not omitted
Format is correct	Format is mostly correct	Format is somewhat correct	Format is not correct
Notes are legible	Notes are mostly legible	Notes are somewhat legible	Notes are not legible
Notes are written in own voice	Notes are mostly written in own voice	Notes are somewhat written in own voice	Notes are not written in own voice

Comments:

Analytical Paragraph Rubric

Advanced	Proficient	Basic	Needs Improvement
First sentence is a clear, specific argument that effectively answers the question	First sentence is a mostly clear, specific argument that mostly effectively answers the question	First sentence is a somewhat clear, specific argument that somewhat effectively answers the question	First sentence is not a clear, specific argument and does not effectively answer the question
Detailed, accurate evidence helps prove the argument	Mostly detailed, accurate evidence helps prove the argument	Somewhat detailed, accurate evidence helps prove the argument	No or little detailed, accurate evidence that doesn't help prove the argument
Thorough analysis woven throughout or included at end	Mostly thorough analysis woven throughout or included at end	Somewhat thorough analysis woven throughout or included at end	No or little analysis woven throughout or included at end
Correct use of language, grammar, style	Mostly correct use of language, grammar, style	Somewhat correct use of language, grammar, style	Incorrect use of language, grammar, style

Comments:

Analytical Essay Rubric

Advanced	Proficient	Basic	Needs Improvement
Thesis is a clear, specific argument that effectively answers the question	Thesis is a mostly clear, specific argument that mostly effectively answers the question	Thesis is a somewhat clear, specific argument that answers the question	Thesis isn't a clear, specific argument and does not effectively answer the question
Detailed, accurate evidence helps prove the argument	Mostly detailed, accurate evidence helps prove the argument	Somewhat detailed, accurate evidence helps prove the argument	No or little detailed, accurate evidence that doesn't help prove the argument
Thorough analysis effectively shows how evidence helps prove argument	Mostly thorough analysis mostly effectively shows how evidence helps prove argument	Somewhat thorough analysis shows how evidence helps prove argument	Analysis doesn't show how evidence helps prove argument
Organization helps prove point	Organization mostly helps prove point	Organization somewhat helps prove point	Organization does not help prove point

Comments:

Research Paper Rubric

Advanced	Proficient	Basic	Needs Improvement
Engaging title and informative subtitle	Mostly engaging title and informative subtitle	Somewhat engaging title and informative subtitle	Unengaging title and uninformative subtitle
Introduction is engaging	Introduction is mostly engaging	Introduction is somewhat engaging	Introduction is not engaging
Introduction includes appropriate background and context	Introduction mostly includes appropriate background and context	Introduction somewhat includes appropriate background and context	Introduction doesn't include appropriate background and context
Thesis is clear, argumentative, meaningful, and precise	Thesis is mostly clear, argumentative, meaningful, and precise	Thesis is somewhat clear, argumentative, meaningful, and precise	Thesis isn't clear, argumentative, meaningful, and precise
Structure and organization add to meaning	Structure and organization mostly add to meaning	Structure and organization somewhat add to meaning	Structure and organization don't add to meaning
Detailed, accurate evidence helps prove the argument	Detailed, accurate evidence mostly helps prove the argument	Detailed, accurate evidence somewhat helps prove the argument	Incomplete, inaccurate evidence doesn't help prove the argument
Thorough analysis shows how evidence helps prove argument	Mostly thorough analysis shows how evidence helps prove argument	Somewhat thorough analysis shows how evidence helps prove argument	Superficial analysis doesn't show how evidence helps prove argument
Conclusion sums up main arguments, raises new issues	Conclusion mostly sums up main arguments, raises new issues	Conclusion somewhat sums up main arguments, raises new issues	Conclusion doesn't sum up main arguments or raise new issues
Appropriate length	Mostly appropriate length	Somewhat appropriate length	Too short in length
Correct in-text citations and Works Cited	Mostly correct in-text citations and Works Cited	Somewhat correct in-text citations and Works Cited	Incorrect in-text citations and Works Cited

Comments:

Book Review Rubric

Advanced	Proficient	Basic	Needs Improvement
Clear summary, without giving too much away	Mostly clear summary, without giving too much away	Somewhat clear summary, without giving too much away	Unclear summary, giving too much away
Main characters, themes, ideas clearly introduced	Main characters, themes, ideas mostly clearly introduced	Main characters, themes, ideas somewhat clearly introduced	Main characters, themes, ideas not clearly introduced
Critical evaluation of text addresses both content and how book was written	Critical evaluation of text mostly addresses both content and how book was written	Critical evaluation of text somewhat addresses both content and how book was written	Uncritical evaluation of text does not address both content and how book was written
Personal evaluation of text connects own thoughts, feelings, experiences to the book	Personal evaluation of text mostly connects own thoughts, feelings, experiences to the book	Personal evaluation of text somewhat connects own thoughts, feelings, experiences to the book	Personal evaluation of text does not connect own thoughts, feelings, experiences to the book
Correct use of language, grammar, style	Mostly correct use of language, grammar, style	Somewhat correct use of language, grammar, style	Incorrect use of language, grammar, style
Publisher, price, and ISBN included at end	Publisher, price, and ISBN mostly included at end	Publisher, price, and ISBN somewhat included at end	Publisher, price, and ISBN missing

Comments:

Dear Students,

It's true that school is—or should be—a meritocracy. But I want you to know that I will be evaluating your *learning*, not you as a person. Please do not associate your achievement with your self-worth. The totality of your human value is not wrapped up in your grade for this class.

I want to tell you what grades mean, and what they don't. Grades are not shorthand for moral value. Those of you who receive higher grades are neither better nor worse *people*—you've just performed better on a particular assignment or over the course of this entire class.

There are many aspects to a life well lived, and social studies achievement is but a sliver. This does not mean you should work any less hard, remain any less engaged, or strive to learn any less than your fullest potential. The reasons for doing your best abound, including understanding yourself and your place in the world, and becoming a more agile thinker and a more capable writer. These pursuits will last a lifetime.

Some of you are funny, some of you play an instrument, others excel in sports or different classes. Some of you speak multiple languages, cook amazing food, and are really good at art. My point is that ALL of you are unique, and ALL of you matter.

Don't let the grades I give you interfere with this fundamental truth. Don't fall into the trap of believing you're valuable or not, worthy or not, according to your ability to write an analytical paragraph or research a primary source. Don't think you're any better or worse people because of the grades you receive. In the end a grade is just an assessment of your knowledge and skills, not a judgement on your character.

Finally, I want you to know that learning is not a fixed character trait. With determination and persistence—and good teaching!—you can all unquestionably improve. Adolescence is not merely about finding something you're good at and sticking with it. (Who even knows what this would be, anyway, as a teenager?) Rather, try to find subjects you enjoy, those that will prove meaningful to your life and to your community.

Every one of us can improve ourselves and our skills. Each of us has the ability to grow. From now on when you receive grades from me, please keep all of this in mind.

Sincerely,

Epilogue

Teachers Are Writers

There are countless reasons why teachers should write, the most direct being that it helps us become better writing teachers. As we know—because we're teachers—people learn best by doing. Action makes learning "sticky." Hence the more we write, the more we are able to help others in turn. Teacher-writing furthers mastery of teaching writing. Experience gives us the confidence to instruct others and the skills to do so effectively. There is simply no substitute.

Yet teachers don't have to be professional writers. They just need to try. Consider keeping a journal; updating a blog; starting a site-based teachers-only magazine; pen an op-ed to a local newspaper; write an article for an organization like EdWeek, Edutopia, or Scholastic.

My first book *Pitching in the Promised Land* originated from a journal I kept while playing baseball in Israel. The journal was far from traditional— I just wrote emails to myself over the course of the season and afterward, because of the madness that was the first (and only) season of professional baseball in the country's history, I knew there was a story to tell. So I wrote, and wrote and wrote and wrote, and revised and edited and tweaked and scrubbed and polished and eventually found an editor at the University of Nebraska Press who wanted to publish my manuscript. Since then, I have been unable to stop.

The point of this anecdote is to illustrate how writing may start out as one thing and end up as another entirely. There's no way around the work—but if one enjoys writing as I certainly do, it ceases to be work at all. It might even become an obsession.

For those who are not passionate about writing that's fine too. It's still worth picking up a pen or pecking at a keyboard from time to time. Recall the title of chapter 2 is "Writing Is Thinking," and while it deals with annotating, notetaking, and reading, it well could have—perhaps should have—also discussed the many benefits writing has on the brain.

In my own personal development I have found that writing has made me a more coherent thinker as well as a less-clumsy public speaker. There is no bullshit detector as effective as the blank page. It forces one to assemble their thoughts in a way they otherwise would not, creating a more organized brain in the process. This at least in theory leads to more effective verbal communication as well. The blank page cannot prevent drivel or clap-trap, but it does provide a tremendous opportunity for intellectual growth.

If these rationales are still unconvincing, how about the desire to share your opinion? You really don't have any beliefs about education from which others wouldn't benefit? The outside world should hear more from teachers, not less. There is so much misinformation about education, so many reductive stereotypes about teachers, that every American, every parent, voter, and policy maker deserves to know the truth.

Inspired by this notion I wrote my second book, *Teacherland,* with the hope of shining some much needed sunlight on the hidden yet consequential concerns of our profession. So speak with your colleagues in the lunchroom; educate your students and maybe even their parents. But don't stop there— share your ideas with the public by writing them down.

Lastly, I'll leave you with one final anecdote. I have a police-officer friend, a former marine, who did not care much for school. Rather than go to college, he enlisted in the military and served several tours in Iraq and Afghanistan before a local police department considered his experience tantamount to a degree and hired him without one. Now guess what he does? He writes. A lot. Ten percent of his time is devoted to "fun stuff," he says, and the other ninety to documenting it.

He compiles police reports of burglarized homes and vandalized businesses. He types out search warrants several thousand words long only to be instructed by the district attorney to provide more detail and more thorough evidence in order to meet the standard of probable cause. Then he comes to my street law class and carps to students about how it's impossible to escape the persuasive essay—at which I grin like a fool. Sometimes it's the messenger, not the message. If teenagers won't listen to their teacher about the importance of writing, maybe they'll learn it from a cop.

I think: in what strange universe do police officers write more than teachers? Sure it's a job requirement for them, though sometimes I wonder if it should also be compulsory for us. An on-demand writing sample was part of my district's application process several decades ago, and it's about the only thing that has remained the same today. We must demonstrate we can write in order to teach but aside from a well-crafted email to parents indicating you are in control of your words and by association also their children, there's little more we're obliged to produce.

Requirements aside, there is so very much to love about writing. It helps us understand ourselves and make sense of our place in this world; it helps us think and communicate, embrace contradictions, and tolerate ambiguity. Writing is the preeminent medium for sharing our thoughts with the rest of humanity, and those who write are naturally afforded a measure of respect.

It is often said that culture is the sea we swim in because it's all around us inescapably. The same goes for many writers young and old, emerging and veteran—writing is no less than a lifeblood. So jump in, teachers. Experience the exhilaration, reap the benefits and joys. Share the magic with your students. Teach them how to write.

Appendix A

Teacher Tools

This book has been about helping teachers teach writing in social studies. The handouts following each chapter are designed to be distributed directly to students. There are, however, a number of teacher-facing tools which may help with planning and instruction, and they are featured in this appendix.

All teachers design lessons, some more thoroughly than others, but not all teachers explicitly write down their plans. I have found that creating a simple table in a digital document has been the single most important tool at my disposal. Without a calendar I quite possibly would not be able to teach. Accordingly the first three resources are a five-, four-, and three-day planning calendar. Select yours based on the number of times you see each class per week. Expand the margins and the boxes for maximum efficiency, insert links, and keep notes—I use angle brackets like these (<< --- >>) to set off the text—for revisions in future years.

The next three tools are the Writing Skills Planning Guide, the Writing Skills Checklist, and the Research Paper Checklist. In the same way we identify content objectives for a unit, semester, and year, we should also do the same for writing. Use the Planning Guide to think through your writing goals at various stages. The Checklist lays out all writing skills in one place; feel free to cross them off as you introduce each to your class. Same goes for the Research Paper Checklist. Since a research paper involves around twelve discrete steps, it can be useful to collate them for the purposes of planning and organization.

Once you've identified your goals, use the Writing Skills Pacing Guide template to map them out. Ideally you'll teach them in the order of the Checklist, at least when it comes to academic writing. You might front-load more of the skills in your first unit and then teach one or two each subsequent unit after that. The sample Writing Skills Pacing Guide offers one such year-long approach.

The next three resources are all about you. About *you* as a writer. The first is the Writing Self-Assessment. Fill it out or simply reflect on the questions as you walk through nature or the city. What type of writer are you? What are your strengths and weaknesses? Following the Self-Assessment, Writing Reflections asks you to dig a bit deeper. Think about specific examples of your writing and think outside the box about what type of writer you might like to become. Have some fun with it. Try to find the joy you'd like to share with your students. Perhaps this means starting a journal—like the Daily Diary Day One.

Finally, one last offering which is meant for students but helps immensely with advanced planning. A unit map is essentially a fancy phrase for a study guide, but one you give students at the beginning of a unit rather than the end. But more than simply listing what terms students will need to recall for a test, a unit map includes both what students will need to know and be able to do. It should feature a combination of the big ideas and key supporting details, as well as an essential question or unifying theme, in addition to the particular academic skills students will be practicing and the summative assessments—like a project and a test—on which they'll be graded.

A sample industrialization unit map from world history is included along with a template for creating your own. These unit maps crystalize the learning objectives for students. They will know exactly where they are going if not explicitly how they will get there. Some students even check supporting details off the list as they encounter them in each lesson. Regardless, unit maps are a helpful tool for teacher planning and student clarity alike. And by including academic skills like source analysis, writing, or speaking directly on the document, students will come to understand the importance of learning skills in addition to content—which has been the primary thrust of this entire book.

Five-Class per Week Planning Calendar

Monday	Tuesday	Wednesday	Thursday	Friday

Four-Class per Week Planning Calendar

Day One	Day Two	Day Three	Day Four

Three-Class per Week Planning Calendar

Day One	Day Two	Day Three

Writing Skills Planning Guide

Year-Long Goals: _____

_____

_____

_____

_____

_____

First Semester Goals: _____

_____

_____

_____

_____

Second Semester Goals: _____

_____

_____

_____

_____

_____

Unit Goals: _____

_____

_____

_____

_____

_____

Weekly Goals: _____

_____

_____

_____

_____

Daily Goals: _____

_____

_____

_____

_____

Writing Skills Checklist
Check each box once you have taught the particular skill. Note that all academic writing should be considered mandatory while real-world writing is à la carte.

Academic Writing

• Annotating
• Notetaking
• Summary
• Source Analysis
• Analytical Paragraph
• Thesis
• Analytical Essay
• Document-Based Question
• Research Paper

Read-World Writing

• Op-Ed
• Book Review
• Historical Fiction Essay
• Magazine Project
• White Paper
• Legal Brief
• Family History Research Project
• Memoir
• Speech
• Visual Essay
• Comics

Research Paper Checklist
*Cross each off once you have begun the particular phase of the research
paper process.*

- Select a topic
- Develop a research question
- Decide on a notetaking style
- Conduct research
- Review paraphrasing versus direct quotes
- Review source evaluation techniques
- Craft a thesis
- Make an outline
- Review citation methods
- Write the first draft
- Edit and revise
- Produce a final copy

Sample Writing Skills Pacing Guide

Consider teaching these skills in the following order. Remember that each is composed of a number of discrete subskills.

Per Unit	Per Semester
Unit One:	Semester One:
Annotating	Annotating
Notetaking	Notetaking
Summary	Summary
Unit Two:	Source Analysis
Source Analysis	Analytical Paragraph
Analytical Paragraph	Analytical Essay
Unit Three:	Semester Two:
Analytical Essay	Document-Based Question
Unit Four:	Research Paper
Document-Based Question	
Unit Five:	
Research Paper	

Writing Skills Pacing Guide Template

Use this form to help determine which skills you will teach in each unit and semester.

Per Unit	Per Semester
Unit One:	Semester One:
Unit Two:	
Unit Three:	
	Semester Two:
Unit Four:	
Unit Five:	

Writing Self-Assessment

Answer the questions below as honestly as you can. You need not show the results to anyone. (You might even consider creating a similar assignment for students.)

What kind of writer are you? _____

_____

_____

_____

_____

What is your writing style? _____

_____

_____

_____

_____

What are your strengths as a writer? _____

_____

_____

_____

What are your weaknesses as a writer? _____

_____

_____

_____

What is your favorite type of writing? _____

_____

_____

_____

What is your least-favorite type of writing? _____

_____

_____

_____

On a scale of 1–10, evaluate your abilities as a writer. Explain. _____

_____

_____

_____

_____

Writing Reflections
Use the space below to think about your past and envision your future.
What is the best thing you've ever written? What are you most proud of?

_____

_____

_____

_____

If you had to be a professional writer, what type of writer would you be? ____

_____

_____

_____

_____

What are your best memories from writing in high school? _____

_____

_____

_____

What are your worst memories from writing in high school? _____

_____

_____

_____

If you had to write a novel, what would it be about? _____

_____

_____

_____

_____

If you had to write about your teaching career, what would you say?

_____

_____

_____

_____

Have you ever kept a diary or journal? Explain. _____

_____

_____

_____

_____

Daily Diary Day One

Welcome to the first day of your diary. Write whatever you want, as much or as little as you'd like. If you'd prefer, digitize this document, store it in the cloud, and type on a mobile device. Or buy a fancy leather journal and enjoy the touch and the smell. Just be sure to write. Every day.

_____

_____

_____

_____

_____

_____

_____

_____

_____

_____

_____

_____

_____

_____

_____

_____

_____

_____

_____

_____

_____

_____

_____

_____

_____

_____

_____

_____

_____

_____

_____

_____

_____

_____

_____

_____

_____

Unit Map: Industrialization
This is what you will need to know and be able to do.

Essential Question: Is technology good?

Big Ideas

- Industrialization shifted the global balance of power
- Industrialization led to political, economic, and social reforms
- Industrialization greatly affected the natural environment
- Technological advancements continue to shape our lives, our country, and our planet

Supporting Details

- Life in Preindustrial England
- Agricultural Revolution
- Seed Drill
- Crop Rotation
- Enclosure Movement
- Factors of Production
- Textile Inventions
- Factories
- Inventions in Transportation
- Entrepreneur
- Steam Engine
- Urbanization
- Puddling Process
- Child Labor
- Laissez-faire
- Capitalism
- Adam Smith
- Thomas Malthus
- David Ricardo
- Utilitarianism
- Jeremy Bentham
- John Stuart Mill
- Utopianism
- Robert Owen
- Socialism
- Communism
- Karl Marx

- Friedrich Engels
- Proletariat
- Bourgeoisie
- Union
- Collective Bargaining
- Strike
- Combination Acts
- American Federation of Labor
- Factory Act
- White Lung and Black Lung
- Rickets
- Mines Act
- Ten Hours Act
- Abolition of Slavery
- Greenhouse Effect
- Ozone Depletion
- Air Pollution
- Water Pollution
- Sustainable Development
- Renewable/Nonrenewable Energy
- Solutions to Environmental Danger

Skills

- Analytical Essay Writing
- Public Speaking

Tasks

- Test (essay, multiple choice, matching, sequence of events)
- Speech

Unit Map:
This is what you will need to know and be able to do.

Essential Question:

Big Ideas

-
-
-
-
-
-

Supporting Details

-
-
-
-
-
-

Skills

-
-
-
-
-
-

Tasks

-
-
-
-
-
-

Appendix B
Q&A

DO YOU ACTUALLY TEACH EVERYTHING
IN THIS BOOK IN YOUR CLASSES?

Yes! Well, no. I teach all of the academic writing every year in every core class—be it U.S. history, world history, government, economics, or geography. I tend to pick and choose from the real-world writing options depending on the particular course since some disciplines lend themselves more naturally to some assignments. I teach less writing in electives like law, psychology, and contemporary world issues.

HAVE YOU ALWAYS TAUGHT THIS WAY?

I have always believed in the importance of teaching skills like reading, writing, and speaking, but early in my career I did not have the tools to do so as effectively or intentionally. There was also a time when this sort of instruction became quite difficult against the backdrop of high-stakes testing pegged to teacher evaluations.

One day a teacher-friend recommended The Global Achievement Gap *by Tony Wagner, which argues for the importance of teaching skills through content, and I think reading this book gave the younger me permission to dive headlong into this type of instruction. Basically, in my bones I've always felt it was best for students, but I've not always lived up to my pedagogical aspirations. I'm heartened that lately there has come to be an emphasis on academic and discipline-specific skills in social studies, which has fueled my desire to write this book.*

HOW AM I SUPPOSED TO TEACH SO MUCH WRITING IN ADDITION TO CONTENT?

I know, right? I think about this question all the time. Sooner or later I remember that skills are equally as important as content. Perhaps a better way of saying it is that the skills are *the content. We all know the old saw: give a person a fish, they eat for a day; teach that person to fish, they eat for a lifetime. Most of us will never forget how to ride a bike, but those of us living outside the Mount Rushmore State have already forgotten that South Dakota's capital is Pierre.*

Writing also helps lodge content in students' brains. We tend to remember more of something when we write about it, so think of the additional minutes spent teaching students how to evaluate a source or craft a thesis as an investment in your content, one that will pay dividends for years to come. How to teach so much writing? Build it in, make it a priority, and have confidence that it will only reinforce the subject matter we're all trying so desperately to convey.

IS WRITING MORE IMPORTANT THAN OTHER SKILLS?

If I had to pick one skill to teach to students, it would either be writing or source evaluation. There are few things as liberating and powerful as learning to write, and there are few as essential as learning to question a source for its veracity. Fortunately, there is a way to square this circle: teach students how to identify bias, perspective, and purpose in both primary and secondary sources as part of your year-long writing skills progression. And feel good about creating a more healthy democracy in the process.

Of course, reading and speaking are also essential skills, ones we should certainly teach in our classes; ones without which our courses would be incomplete. But as they are not the subject of this book, I have chosen a different answer (see, bias is inescapable).

HOW OFTEN SHOULD STUDENTS WRITE?

I really believe students should be writing every week, if not every day. Writing is not just a skill students develop in the abstract—it reinforces the content, allowing students to engage more deeply with the key learnings of your class. More time spent writing is not less time learning history, government, or geography. Quite the opposite, in fact.

And remember you don't need to grade, or even look at, every piece of student work. Much of the day-to-day writing students should think of as practice. This might include outlining a DBQ (document-based question), summarizing a reading, or revising an analytical paragraph.

REALLY, STUDENTS SHOULD WRITE EVERY WEEK IF NOT EVERY DAY?

Yes! There are outward limits, of course, and the slippery slope argument still applies. Students should not write excessively to the exclusion of everything else; they still need to converse, argue, and debate, watch movies, engage in simulations, draw, act, etcetera. Teaching students to write is integral to teaching social studies, but it is by no means the sole instructional strategy at our disposal. Mix it up, but don't forget to mix it in.

SHOULD STUDENTS WRITE FOR HOMEWORK?

Ah, homework. One of many pedagogical landmines we must navigate. My simple overarching answer is that homework is often necessary, but the least possible amount is preferable. In social studies, students regularly read at home in order to come to class ready to discuss and apply what they have learned. Students most commonly annotate or take notes, which are forms of writing themselves (even if they happen to be reading strategies, specifically).

When assigning summative writing assignments like process pieces, especially those requiring research, whatever students aren't able to finish in class can be done at home in advance of the due date. Students might also take additional time to prepare for an in-class essay. But in the big picture, try to keep homework to a minimum.

HOW DO I TEACH WRITING WHEN I DON'T FEEL LIKE A COMPETENT WRITER MYSELF?

Good question. Try to forget the adage that those who can, do, and those who can't, teach. As with coaches, it's often helpful to have some personal experience but certainly not necessary—not every teacher and coach has achieved at exceptionally high levels themselves and that's okay. Nonetheless, some fluency with the written word can only help. Confidence in writing will lead to confidence in teaching writing, which is why I believe it's so helpful for teachers to be writers. Or at least to write regularly.

There are a number of organizations devoted to this ideal, like the National Writing Project. I have attended workshops with the Bay Area Writing Project, the National Writing Project's founding branch, and I always come away feeling energized and optimistic. There are almost 200 affiliates nationwide and I highly recommend you give one a try. But even if you don't, you can still write on your own. You'll gain confidence simply by putting words on the page.

DID YOU REALLY GET THE IDEA FOR THIS BOOK FROM A COOKBOOK ABOUT TACOS?

I did—true story. I'd been turning this project over in my mind for a while, but it wasn't until I picked up the cookbook that the concept crystalized for me. I enjoy cooking but don't feel especially confident, in part because I lack formal training. At once informative and engaging, motivating and accessible, the cookbook gave me the conviction and the tools to experiment with new techniques. Once I learned how to properly hand press masa, I became obsessed with mastering the craft. One man's corn tortilla, I hope, is another person's thesis.

HOW SHOULD I USE THE STUDENT HANDOUTS YOU'VE INCLUDED?

Any way you'd like. Make photocopies directly from the book and distribute them to students, or create digital files and personalize them, make them your own. I usually feel most comfortable giving students handouts that sound like me, but I've also stolen plenty from my colleagues verbatim. So you might consider a combination of the two.

WHAT'S UP WITH THE FORMATTING OF THE HANDOUTS?

Because of the publishing exigencies of typesetting, the process of arranging text on a page, it's difficult if not impossible to create a more advanced layout. The handouts I use with my own classes take advantage of hard spaces, thinner margins, and a variety of other tricks to make them more visually appealing. Think about doing the same with yours.

DOES IT MATTER IF MY STUDENTS ARE HIGH-SKILLED OR LOW-SKILLED OR IF THERE'S A WIDE VARIATION IN STUDENT ABILITY?

Yes and no. Ability should not prevent students from participating in any particular assignment. In fact the lower one's skill, arguably, the more urgent the need to teach them how to write, and to provide ample opportunities to practice. But pacing and instruction should always be tailored to the kids in the room, so it makes sense that some classes may take longer to complete a research paper or write an in-class DBQ essay, with additional scaffolding along the way. Think back to the framework—explain, model, practice, give feedback, practice—and lengthen the depth of support as necessary for every step in the process.

The trickiest classes are often those with a wide cleft in skill level. Some students need very little instruction and are ready to run straight out of the gate, while others require more monitoring and personal interaction. This is what it means to teach, and teach well. If I knew any better, I wouldn't say ours is one of the hardest professions in the world. But I don't, so I do.

WHAT ROLE DO FACTORS LIKE RACE AND SOCIOECONOMIC STATUS PLAY?

They play a massive role in education. We have such a weighty responsibility to ensure our students are cared for and loved, that they feel safe, supported, and secure. We also have the power to help create a more just society by allowing for fair equality of opportunity in our classrooms. Regardless of the color of a student's skin or the income of their parents, or for that matter their religion, political preference, or sexual orientation, all kids can learn to write. All kids can discover the power of the written word.

SHOULD I BE CONCERNED ABOUT NEGATIVE FEEDBACK FROM PARENTS?

No. I understand this is a practical reality, especially for younger teachers, but I have rarely if ever encountered parents who wish their kids wrote less. *Attentive parents care about student workloads, wanting to ensure assignments are relevant and worthwhile. Leaving aside the hot poker that is communicating grades, you should not have to worry about parents complaining that their kids write too much. If anything, in the aggregate, parents may grumble about students writing too little.*

HOW DID YOU FIND TIME TO WRITE A
BOOK WHILE ALSO TEACHING?

I wrote most of the manuscript for this book before the birth of my son. In my pre-parenthood life I'd write on weekends and breaks, and often on school nights. I suppose it's the same now, albeit with way less time. But I try to remind myself there's no excuse and that those who want to write, write. Finding time between planning and grading can be difficult. If that all seems like too much, consider starting with breaks and the summer and see if you gather momentum that may propel you into the school year.

DID YOU FOLLOW ANY OF THESE
WRITING TIPS YOURSELF?

Yes, many. This book began with an idea which wormed its way inside my head and wouldn't leave: that there should be more resources dedicated to helping social studies teachers teach writing. Eventually, the idea grew too large and I had to write it down. Some months of brainstorming led to a skeletal outline, the bones of which I fleshed out over the course of a year or two. For me this was the hardest part, the blank page. After an initial draft came countless hours editing, which I mostly enjoyed, because I was able to see the work come to life.

Looking back, the writing process I teach to students—brainstorm, outline, write a first draft, revise, and polish—is exactly the template I have followed here.

WHAT SHOULD I DO WHEN I KEEP
GETTING PUSHBACK FROM STUDENTS
FOR ASKING THEM TO WRITE?

Ooh! the huffing and puffing. In my experience there are few times in the classroom when students expunge as much hot air as when you inform them of an upcoming essay. The collective expiration could levitate a blimp.

You might make fun of them, in a tender, loving sort of way, or just explain your rationale for the assignment. Some things in life are hard, and most of the accomplishments we're truly proud of take effort. For students with an extracurricular passion, like sports or music, ask them how often they practice, how frequently they're required to drill the fundamentals in preparation for a concert or game.

Or give them a pep talk about the power of the written word, about how much better prepared they'll be for college, how much more hireable they'll appear to future employers, how much money, fame, influence, love, and admiration they'll gain, all thanks to your amazing assignment. You might throw in that you agree with them, you know writing is difficult, especially getting started, you've been in that position more times than you can count— not just as a student but all those many occasions you've had to write in your life as an adult. But ideally, and here's the trick, work is no longer work when it becomes something you love.

In short, acknowledge how they're feeling, remind them why it's so important to write, and mix in some humor and inspiration as you see fit.

WHY DO STUDENTS SEEM TO DISLIKE WRITING?

Great question. I'm not sure students dislike writing, really, but my suspicion is that a lot of their fear and anxiety is tied to the pressure surrounding grades. Plus writing is hard—it's mentally taxing and there are plenty of easier things to do. I also wonder if students are put off by the rigid nature of exposition, à la the five-paragraph essay, and the feeling that they can never write about subjects that matter personally to them. Which is all the more reason, of course, to emphasize real-world writing and to design assignments requiring students to connect the curriculum to their lives and the present day.

CAN STUDENTS WRITE ON THEIR PHONES?

Yes. Students, like all of us, can write anywhere. Make notes, jot down fragments of an idea, store your documents in the cloud, and write wherever you can. For genuine composition, a computer—or heaven forfend a stack of paper—is clearly preferable. But any technology, anything that encourages students to write, is a positive. (I would not recommend students write on their phones in class, however, since other options exist.)

HOW DO SOCIAL MEDIA AND THE
INTERNET AFFECT STUDENT WRITING?

Both social media and the internet are powerful distractions that rob us of deep thought. There is a direct link between boredom and creativity. The mind must wander if it is to get anywhere at all. If there is no time to think, there is certainly no time to write. We'd all be well served to use both social media and the internet, especially the former, in smaller doses.

That said if kids are texting and posting and commenting about any number of topics using words, and not solely images or emoji, then social media and by extension the internet can actually enhance students' command of language. Students can write informally, in the same manner that some people code switch, as long as they know when it's best to use one way of communicating over another. The classroom and the hallways are two very different spaces indeed.

HOW CAN I COLLABORATE MORE WITH
MY COLLEAGUES AROUND WRITING?

Tough one. Most schools' schedules simply aren't set up for real collaboration, which means we're constantly swimming upstream. Make use of the few hours set aside each month outside of staff meetings, be it in pairs or with your entire department. Think about aligning skills vertically between all grade levels, perhaps even in a progression, as well as about horizontal consistency among teachers of like classes. If you bristle at this sort of alignment, you might at least benefit from knowing what your colleagues are doing.

There's so little time to collaborate, but being part of a team can feel nothing less than rejuvenating. It can inspire us to test out new approaches and resist the lure of curricular stagnation. And it can remind us that we're not in it alone, that we all struggle with knowing what types of writing to assign and how much, what particular instructional techniques are most effective and how much feedback one teacher can possibly give.

Not that I'm recommending it, but if you're able to do this with your peers on your prep periods or before or after school, you are nothing less than a hero in my book. Teaching can be a lonely profession, and collaboration (as well as eating lunch with friends) is often the best antidote.

SERIOUSLY, I'M SUPPOSED TO TEACH
ALL THIS WRITING AND CONTENT
AND A HOST OF OTHER SKILLS?

Yes! It's a really tricky dance, determining the right balance between content and academic skills. Just remember: skills through content. This is key. We cannot teach it all, so we have to prioritize and make decisions about what is essential. For me, this means using the subject matter of a course to teach students how to read, write, and speak—as well as how to think.

DOES OUR PROFESSIONAL ORGANIZATION
HAVE ANYTHING TO SAY ABOUT THIS?

*Yes. The National Council for Social Studies (NCSS) has published The C3 Framework (*The College, Career, and Civic Life (C3) Framework for Social Studies State Standards: Guidance for Enhancing the Rigor of K-12 Civics, Economics, Geography, and History*) which aims among other things to highlight the primacy of skills like writing in our disciplines. It's a helpful guide and illustrates yet again how social studies is about much more than learning content.*

And by the way if you are not a member of NCSS I recommend you join. Membership in this national organization reinforces the professional nature of our careers and illustrates the need to continually learn and grow—just as we ask of our students.

IF I FORGET EVERYTHING I'VE JUST READ
IN THIS BOOK BUT REMEMBER ONLY
ONE THING, WHAT SHOULD IT BE?

Teach students to write. You know how. Now is the time to do it.

Appendix C

Suggested Reading

I. THE WRITING CRAFT

Arana, Marie. *The Writing Life: Writers on How They Think and Work*. Public Affairs, 2003.

Bradbury, Ray. *Zen in the Art of Writing*. Bantam Books, 1992.

Dillard, Annie. *The Writing Life*. Harper Perennial, 2013.

Fish, Stanley Eugene. *How to Write a Sentence and How to Read One*. Harper Paperbacks, 2012.

Hale, Constance. *Sin and Syntax: How to Craft Wicked Good Prose*. Three River, 2013.

King, Stephen. *On Writing: A Memoir of the Craft*. Pocket Books, 2002.

Klinkenborg, Verlyn. *Several Short Sentences about Writing*. Vintage Books, 2013.

Kramer, Mark, and Wendy Call. *Telling True Stories: A Nonfiction Writer's Guide from the Nieman Foundation at Harvard University*. Plume, 2007.

Lamott, Anne. *Bird by Bird: Some Instructions on Writing and Life*. Anchor Books, 2019.

Pinker, Steven. *The Sense of Style: The Thinking Person's Guide to Writing in the 21st Century*. Penguin Books, 2015.

Pressfield, Steven. *The War of Art: Break through the Blocks and Win Your Inner Creative Battles*. Black Irish Entertainment, 2012.

Strunk, William, et al. *The Elements of Style*. Penguin Books, 2007.

Williams, Joseph M. *Style: Ten Lessons in Clarity and Grace*. Longman, 2000.

Zinsser, William. *On Writing Well: The Classic Guide to Writing Nonfiction*. Harper Perennial, 2016.

II. GRAMMAR AND USAGE

Fogarty, Mignon. *Grammar Girl's Quick and Dirty Tips for Better Writing*. St. Martin's Griffin, 2008.

Norris, Mary. *Between You & Me: Confessions of a Comma Queen*. W.W. Norton and Company, 2016.

Straus, Jane, et al. *The Blue Book of Grammar and Punctuation*. John Wiley & Sons, 2014.

Truss, Lynne. *Eats, Shoots & Leaves: The Zero Tolerance Approach to Punctuation*. Gotham Books, 2006.

III. CITATION AND STYLE

American Psychological Association. *Publication Manual of the American Psychological Association*. Seventh ed., American Psychological Association, 2019.

The Associated Press. *The Associated Press Stylebook 2019: And Briefing on Media Law*. Basic Books, 2019.

The Modern Language Association of America. *MLA Handbook*. Eighth ed., Modern Language Association of America, 2016.

The University of Chicago Press Editorial Staff. *The Chicago Manual of Style*. Seventeenth ed., University of Chicago Press, 2017.

IV. MISCELLANEOUS

Booth, Wayne et al. *The Craft of Research*. Chicago, 2003.

Lopate, Phillip. *To Show and to Tell: The Craft of Literary Nonfiction*. Free Press, 2013.

McWhorter, John. *Lexicon Valley: A Podcast About Language, From Pet Peeves to Syntax*. Podcast audio. Slate. https://slate.com/podcasts/lexicon-valley.

National Council for the Social Studies. "C3 Framework." *National Council for the Social Studies*, 2019, www.socialstudies.org/c3.

Purdue Writing Lab. *Purdue Writing Lab*, 2019, owl.purdue.edu.

UNC-Chapel Hill Writing Center. *The Writing Center*, 2019, writingcenter.unc.edu.

Orwell, George. *Politics and the English Language*. Penguin, 2013.

Seixas, Peter, and Tom Morton. *The Big Six Historical Thinking Concepts*. Nelson Education, 2013.

About the Author

Aaron Pribble is the author of *Teacherland: Inside the Myth of the American Educator* and *Pitching in the Promised Land: A Story of the First and Only Season in the Israel Baseball League.* An award-winning educator, Aaron teaches social studies at Tamalpais High School in Mill Valley, California. He loves tacos and teaching his kids how to write.

www.ingramcontent.com/pod-product-compliance
Lightning Source LLC
Chambersburg PA
CBHW050530270326
41926CB00015B/3155